Navigation Exercises

COLIN JONES

Helmsman Books

First published in 1993 by
Helmsman Books, an imprint of
The Crowood Press Ltd
Ramsbury, Marlborough
Wiltshire SN8 2HR

British Library Cataloguing-in-Publication Data

A catalogue record for this book is available from the British Library

ISBN 1 85223 701 5

Picture credits

Photographs by Colin Jones.
Line-drawings by Claire Upsdale-Jones.

Acknowledgements

The author would like to express thanks and appreciation for the assistance given by the producers of Imray Charts, Reeds Nautical Almanac, and MacMillans and Silk Cut Almanac; and also the many professionals in the marine trade who made helpful suggestions.

Typeset by Avonset, Midsomer Norton, Avon
Printed and bound in Great Britain by BPCC Hazell Books, Aylesbury

CONTENTS

1 The Acquaint Class   5

2 The Compass   7

3 The Marine Chart   21

4 More About the Chart   38

5 High Water and Low Water   44

6 The Tide – For or Against?   52

7 The Ship's Log   62

8 Electronic Navigation   68

9 Let's Go Cruising   76

10 The Rules of the Road   81

11 Let's Have an Adventure   86

12 Final Destination   101

13 Revision Class   102

    Answers to Exercises   114

    Glossary   122

    Index   126

1
THE ACQUAINT CLASS

This is a book for beginners to navigation. I also hope that it will be as versatile as all good boat tools and serve as a refresher course for those whose pilotage skills have become a little rusty, or that it might even form the basis of a syllabus for skippers teaching crews to navigate as they sail their boats from one harbour to another.

The origins of the ideas which follow are both practical and personal. They stem from that far-off time when I knew nothing of the way in which boats find their way around in a medium where there are no road signs and very few landmarks. As a child, I was fascinated by the sheer magic of being able to know where you are and where you are going, even though you can see nothing but a 360 degree, flat and very wet horizon.

At that time, like now, I lived very close to the sea and the cliffs. It was a super place in which to grow up, but was entirely devoid of evening classes and other institutes of further learning. Like most of my friends I therefore learned everything from books, and acquiring new skills became a matter of self-reliance and self-tuition. Books are superb teachers, because they allow you to learn at your own pace and encourage you to repeat those parts which you are finding difficult. There are still no suitable classes in my area, so it was entirely from books that I got through the complexities of the exam for the Radio Amateur's Licence and learned another language when my own cruising boat was headed down for Spain. These and other book-derived skills have remained with me ever since – as has a fascination with maps and charts.

There are those who will say that they do not need to learn traditional pilotage skills because their boat is equipped with so much electronic wizardry that they never get lost, and never need use pencil and paper. Such braggarts could not be more wrong, nor more deprived of some of the best parts of their pastime. Even though we now have marvellous modern navigational instruments with a high degree of automation, we still need to be able to do the basics well. This is not so much because you need to cope with unlikely events of emergency or of electronic breakdown, but simply because you need a good grasp of the fundamentals if you are to get the best out of GPS, Decca, radar, radio, depth-sounders and chart pilots.

There is an educational philosophy which states: 'What I hear I note; those things I read I remember; the things which I actually do remain with me forever.' In essence, this says that the best way to learn is by doing, but in order to do anything you must begin by understanding the principles. The first step is to subject yourself to an explanation of the things which you aim to learn. In short, you read about them.

This is the rationale which has guided the compilation of this book. It takes a look at the separate facets of navigation, and examines each skill which the navigator needs for coastal and trans-Channel passage making. Each component's background theory and foreground, hands-on practice is explained. Each mini-tutorial is then followed by some practical examples to be worked either on paper, with a calculator, or on the chartlets which are sprinkled throughout these pages. In this way you will be able to check that you are correctly transferring theory to reliable practice.

Even if you already understand the basics, practice still makes perfect. If you become automatic in your use of chart and compass in the comfort of your own home, you will be much more efficient when you are out at sea and when you might need to do these things quickly. Besides, if you enjoy your hobby, teaching yourself to navigate at home is another way of extending your love of boats and the sea into the dark nights and through boring, rainy days.

You can start this navigation course with nothing more than a pencil, paper and ruler. If you have a set square and a protractor, you will be able to use them. A set of ordinary geometry set dividers is useful, but you can also use a pair of compasses to do the same thing. Later on, the addition of either a parallel rule or a Breton plotter will considerably increase your enjoyment and make your learning more rapid.

The chartlets in the book have not been taken from anywhere in particular. Most of them have been devised by the editorial team and the descriptions of some of the hazardous passages, like the Raz de Sein, are from my own observations as I made these voyages. The tidal information is similarly contrived as a tutorial vehicle and does not bear any relationship to any particular day, or even to any actual area. The photographs are of the following Imray charts:

C10 – Western English Channel Passage Chart.
C35 – Baie de Morlaix to Aberildut.
C36 – Ile d'Ouessant to Raz de Sein.
C37 – Raz de Sein to Benodet.

If you have these sheets to hand, you will have even more fun and be closer to the real feeling of being responsible for your own boat. The Admiralty practice charts (or any other chart of the same areas) will also serve just as well.

My sincere thanks go to Imray, Laurie, Norie and Wilson for the assistance which they have given in the writing of this book, and for the way they make their charts fold into exactly the right size for the locker in which I keep them on the boat.

The foregoing has been the equivalent of the cruise captain's briefing before the club fleet sets off. I know that I am going to have a lot of fun – and even learn some new skills and ideas – as I compile and write this series of seminars. I wish you the same pleasures.

2
THE COMPASS

A boat without a compass is no boat at all. Some means of verifying your direction of travel really is the most basic and the most frequently used tool on board. Even if your water vehicle is a beach-hugging family runabout, a small compass and the knowledge of how to use it are a good safety factor to have.

The compass has one essential property. It always points to the north and everything else the compass does is derived from that one fact. More basically, it is not the compass which seeks constantly to point to the north no matter how you spin it, but the magnetized bar beneath the graphics card. Tradition says that it was the Chinese who first discovered that lodestone which is floated in water has the peculiar characteristic of always turning to point in the same direction. From that time, progress has used the phenomenon to encapsulate the water in a portable bowl

A compass consists of a card and a magnetized bar.

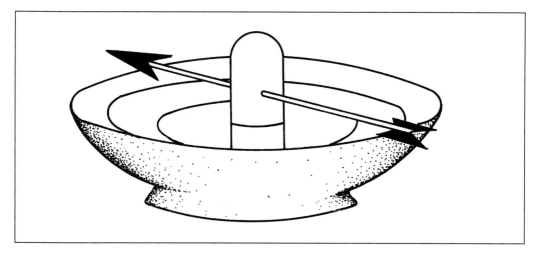

An early compass – lodestone floating on water.

and then to inhibit a too-rapid swing by replacing this fluid with various oils and alcohols. The simple pointer was expanded to show directions off to the side and the piece of lodestone gave way to a magnetized bar.

Compass Terminology

The ordinary magnetic compass has not really changed much since those early days. Even though we have better engineering and very clear compass cards, all navigation still stems from the fact that we can rely on the instrument to point where it has always pointed, and can calculate other directions from this. It does not really matter what you call these other directions as long as everybody understands the terminology employed. International convention decrees that if you move one clockwise right angle from north you will face east, that the six o'clock position shall be called south, and so on. These four cardinal points are abbreviated

to N,S,E and W. If you stop halfway between the N and E right angle, you will be at 45° to N, or at the NE point.

It is interesting to observe here that you are already beginning to speak the

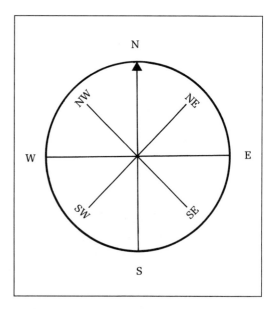

Cardinal and half-cardinal points.

8

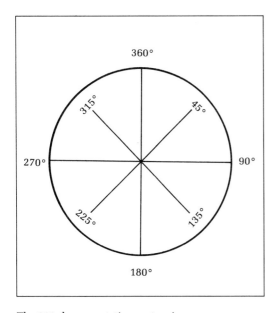

The 360-degree notation system is more modern.

A bearing is more precise in digits.

navigator's working language when using the compass. He speaks of 'points' and 'degrees', which is really a mixture of both ancient and modern terms. Those adventurers who sailed before the mast had to learn how to 'box the compass' – in other words, to recite the thirty-two points into which the compass is divided. A point equals 11.25° or, as defined by an old dictionary, 'the angle of 11 degrees and 15 minutes between two adjacent marks on a compass card'. Along the way, our need for speed has meant that we have dropped such phrases as 'north-north-east by east' and replaced them with the system called 360-degree notation or, sometimes, three-figure notation. Put simply, the circle starts at north or zero and moves via NE at 45°, E at 90°, SE at 135° and so on round the clock to 360° which is the second definition of north. This gives the greater precision which is

needed when you are navigating by radar or using other electronic apparatus, whereby a course as precise as 193° is possible.

In practice, seafarers still tend to use the cardinal and half-cardinal points because they are pictorially simple: 'I am heading NE from the Fairway Buoy', 'the yacht *Eagle* is south of me at the moment', 'the tide will be going north-west from about noon'. This is navigation in its 'coarse tuning mode'. When a more precise measurement is required, however, we change to three-figure language: 'steer one five nine', 'the Fairway Buoy is bearing zero two three from us', 'the course from the end of the breakwater to clear Rock Point is two six four'. Notice that the zero is always included – even in 'zero zero nine' – and that the digits are given separately. A course is never called 'a hundred and sixty-five', but rather 'one six five'.

Exercise 2.1

Give the 360° notation angles for NE, E, SE, S, SW, W, NW, ENE, SSW and NNW. Give your answers in the format NE = 45°, E = 90° and so on, and round them up to the nearest degree.

Measuring a Compass Angle

Measuring an angle at sea is no different from the way in which you were taught to do it at school. The principle is that you put the centre of your circle (protractor) on the 'starting location' and count degrees clockwise from there. Because a seaman's 'starting location' is never fixed, a number of means of making life easier have been devised.

The first of these is the compass rose which is always printed at several convenient places on every chart. This is basically nothing more than a circle, with its centre clearly indicated and its circumference marked off in degrees. To measure a compass angle (which is also called a bearing) you simply join the centre of the circle to your target and take your reading from the point where the joining line cuts the circumference of the circle. In the illustration opposite, if you assume that your boat is positioned at the centre of the compass rose then the headland bears 50° from you, the red can buoy is at 222° and the green triangle buoy is at 310°, with all bearings related to north.

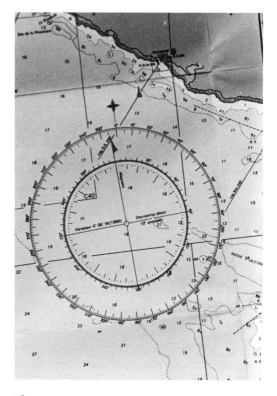

The compass rose.

Exercise 2.2

Use an ordinary ruler to give your skipper the bearing of the five boats surrounding your own as indicated on the illustration opposite. The simplest way to do this on the chart table of a rolling boat is to use the end of a pencil as a pivoting fixed point to hold your ruler in place (*see* the photograph opposite).

Exercise 2.3

Write down or say aloud how you would call the location of each of the targets from Exercise 2.2 from the cockpit to the navigator at his table in the saloon.

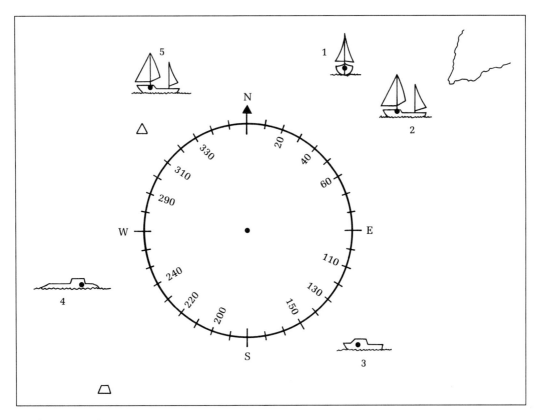

The five-vessel plot.

The ruler pivots on the pencil.

Aboard a yacht on passage, this type of information is passed in order to pinpoint the boat's position on a chart by relating it to channel buoys, headlands and lighthouses. It is also used to plot the course and position of other vessels which might become a collision hazard. The bearings are measured with a hand-portable compass, from the yacht's radar, or using both.

Practical Plotting

In real life, your boat will rarely be located in the precise centre of a compass rose, so we need some means of moving our circle

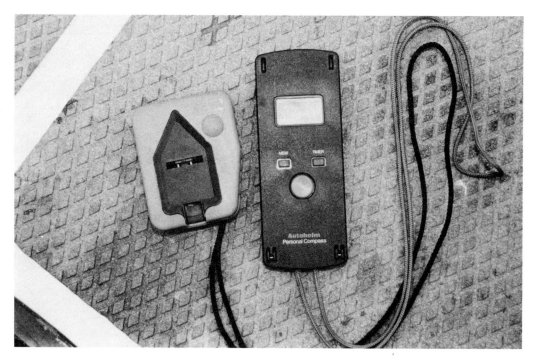

There are many types of hand-held compass.

freely around the chart. As long as we are careful to put its centre on our own boat's position (or buoy) and to align the figure zero with north, we could use an ordinary protractor for this task, or even have a transparent circle and move it around at will. Some skippers still use this as a handy way of plotting bearings when the chart is in a confined space.

The parallel rule achieves the same end more rapidly and sometimes more accurately because it is self-aligning. The principles remain the same as when using an ordinary rule except that the bearing or angle is transferred from the compass rose to another part of the chart, or vice versa.

To use a parallel rule, draw a line from your boat's position as plotted on the chart to the target – say, a buoy or a lighthouse.

The circular protractor.

The edge of the ruler is through the very centre.

Manipulate the rule's hinges to 'walk' the device across the chart until any of its four edges coincides with the centre of the rose and cuts the circumference. You now have your bearing, or the course you will steer to reach your target.

You can use either method (circular protractor or parallel rule) to do Exercise 2.4.

Exercise 2.4

Give the approximate course to steer to reach each of the waypoints on the chartlet overleaf.

1. Can buoy.
2. Starboard marker.
3. Lighthouse.
4. Safe water mark.
5. Port hand marker.
6. Anchorage.
7. Position fix.

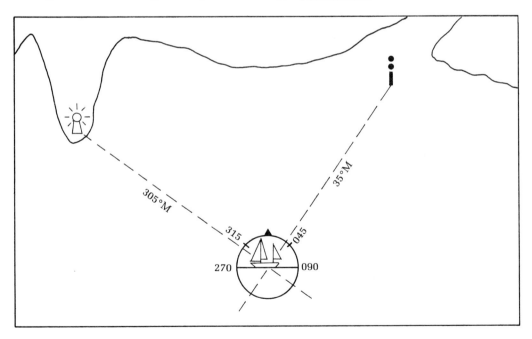

Two bearings give a positional fix.

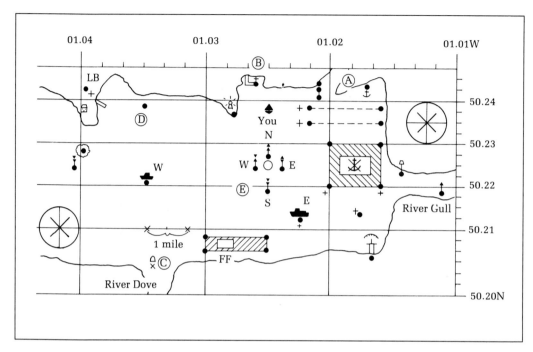

Chart for Exercise 2.4.

Note If you are doing the practice exercises in this book on a commercial chart, you will notice that the compass roses have two annotated circles. For the moment, ignore the inner circle and take all your bearings at the outer.

The Breton plotter is another method of achieving the same result. It is a little more expensive to buy, but is very convenient for use on small or folded charts and does not suffer the slippage errors which may occur when a parallel rule is being moved. Most good navigators have a variety of instruments in their racks.

True or Magnetic?

The magnetized bars beneath the compass

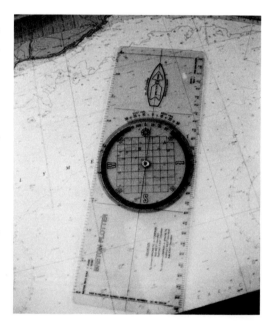

The Breton plotter.

card align themselves with the magnetic pole, which is somewhere to the north of Canada. Unfortunately, this point is not fixed but moves slightly each year. However, its direction and progress can be calculated and this information is printed inside the compass rose. This movement is called the magnetic variation, and is the angle by which magnetic north varies from an arbitrarily fixed position universally known as true north. True north is the point at which the chart's vertical grid lines meet.

Without this fixed position as a permanent reference, all charts would have to be reprinted every year. So, in fact, it makes more sense to say by how much true north varies from magnetic north. It is also essential to know whether this variation is to the left or right, east or west, or clockwise or anticlockwise. (In layman's language these all amount to the same thing.) The variation is called east when it is to the right of the true north line (in other words, towards the east) and west when it is to its left. In the Northern Hemisphere, magnetic deviation is currently west. In simple terms, this means that in order to obtain degrees true (to put on my chart) I must subtract the variation figure from my compass course.

On my desk I have a chart called Imray C15 – The Solent. The compass rose legend says: 'Variation 4° 40'W 1990 decreasing about 10' annually'. These figures will change slightly over the years, and in practice these changes are so slight that they can be ignored. For the record, however, imagine a single degree on the compass rose, split this into sixty minutes, then see if you can visualize what ten of them look like.

The other chart on my desk is the Imray C10 – Western English Channel. This

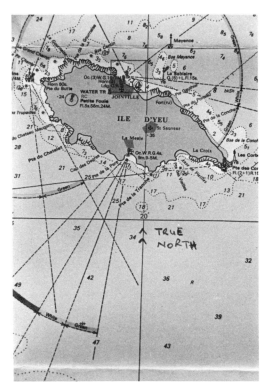

True north coincides with a grid line.

covers a large area and is used for passage planning. Two of its compass roses say: 'A Variation 6° 25'W 1990 decreasing about 10' annually', and 'B Variation 4° 50'W 1990 decreasing about 10' annually'. So, if I am off the western corner of France, I must subtract about 6 degrees from my compass course when I draw the line on the chart. Up near the Channel Islands, the subtraction will be just over 4 degrees.

In practice, nobody can steer a bouncing boat to within a degree, so most navigators would select a figure of 5° for both of these locations, especially as many boat compasses are only marked off in 5° intervals. This figure might need to be altered to take more account of magnetic variation if the

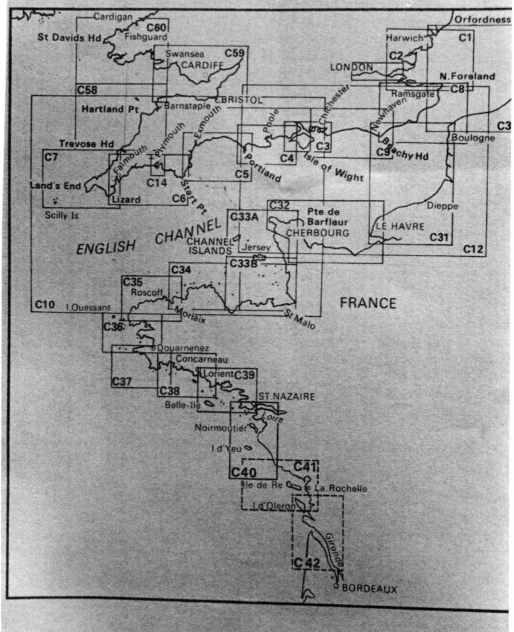

Different charts cover different sea areas.

same chart is used in ten years' time – a very unlikely happening, because so much of the charted information would have rendered the sheet obsolete by that time and, if it has been used properly, it could well have been written on many times over.

Some navigators do not like mental arithmetic, so they always work in magnetic courses and bearings because by doing so they can avoid errors. In my own case, I need to operate both M (magnetic north) and T (true north) because my boat is equipped with both a Decca radio navigator and a GPS (Global Positioning System) satellite position-fixing method. Both of these are universal systems, so all their information is referenced to true north. To avoid confusion, all headings are written with the appropriate letter noted after them – for example, 125°T for true and 237°M for a magnetic bearing read from the compass.

If you are working from the chart to the compass, variation is added. Thus a navigator might call to the helmsman: 'Bearing is 090T. Variation is 6° west. Steer 096.' The method is much easier to do than to explain, but the following exercise will give you some practice.

Exercise 2.5

Assume a magnetic variation of 5°W. You are running a Decca plot, giving information in degrees T. What compass course will your helmsman steer to get you to the waypoints (destinations) concerned?

1.	095T	6.	182T
2.	033T	7.	333T
3.	231T	8.	061T
4.	005T	9.	123T
5.	003T	10.	111T

Exercise 2.6

Assume the local magnetic variation is 7°W. You are out in the fog and are being guided up a channel by a shore-based radar station. He gives you the following courses to steer. What will your compass read each time when you are dead on course?

1.	180T	6.	143T
2.	301T	7.	119T
3.	331T	8.	005T
4.	193T	9.	211T
5.	270T	10.	359T

The Reciprocal

Sometimes a boat will need to reverse its course in order to return to harbour, or even to run back up its own wake to pick up something which has fallen overboard. The simplest way to find a reciprocal bearing is to run the ruler straight across a compass rose and read it from the edge line (see the photograph on page 13).

If you have to find a reciprocal in your head, some numbers will be easy to calculate; others can be simplified by using one of several short cuts. My own short cut for low numbers is to add 200 and take off 20:

The reciprocal of 075T is
075 + 200 = 275 – 20 = 255.

For higher numbers the easy method is to take off 200 and add 20:

The reciprocal of 333T is
333 – 200 = 133 + 20 = 153.

Exercise 2.7

What are the reciprocals of the following?

1.	181T	6.	358T
2.	200T	7.	015T
3.	020T	8.	072M
4.	335M	9.	227T
5.	275M	10.	140T

Compass Deviation

It is a pity that the words deviation and variation are phonetically and etymologically so close to each other that they can cause some confusion. However, if you always remember the terms as 'magnetic variation' and 'compass deviation', you will not get them wrong.

If you look at a batch of three compasses, they might give you three different readings. The discrepancies should only be small, but you should be aware of them. The causes of a compass deviating from a perfectly accurate reading are many, one such cause being inherent faults in on-board equipment creating magnetic fields

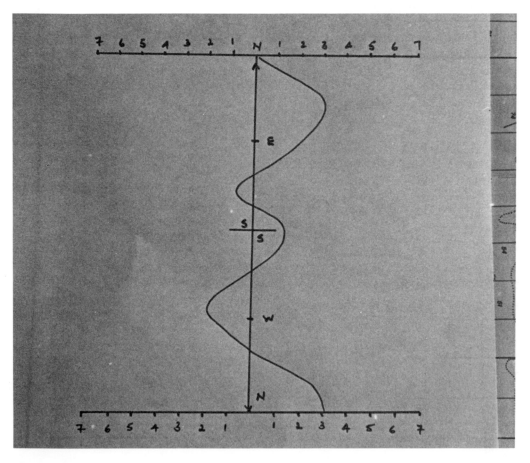

The compass deviation card.

which pull the needle off line. Radio loudspeakers have magnets which also play havoc with compasses. The classic cause, however, is the control panel of a twin-engined boat, which will generally have its compass placed between the two engines and adjusted for balance at installation. If one engine is faulty and has to be shut down, the compass can become useless.

The problem with compass deviation is that it is not standard 'all around the clock'. In practice, many of us simply ignore small aberrations because navigation is a relatively inexact science whose shortcomings are overcome as the navigator uses a variety of tools and systems which check each other out. You should, however, be aware of any compass deviation in case, like me, you have one compass which varies from being 'spot on' at 005 to 7° fast at 170, then comes back to zero fault again.

A well-run boat will have a deviation card available, just like the example in the illustration. The helmsman can then add or subtract as the case might be. My card was built up over the period of a cruise by checking my compass from known positions on the chart to distant objects identified by eye and then located on the chart.

Mastery of the compass is easily the most important of all navigational skills. After all, if you are lost somewhere between England and France, you can be the best chart operator in the world and still not get home. However, if you can read the compass, you will be able to point the boat's head either to north or south and at least be certain of hitting one shore or the other.

All Mariners are Geographers

The First Atlas

The first atlas was created when the Flemish geographer Gerhardus Mercator put together a book of maps whose frontispiece was a picture of the God Atlas supporting the world on his shoulders, just as he does in the ancient legend. Since that time any collection of maps has come to be known as an atlas.

The Longest Possible Voyage

To make the longest possible sea voyage on earth start 150 miles west of Karachi (Pakistan) go via the Mozambique Channel, on to the Drake Passage, then up to the Bering Sea to reach your final destination at a point 200 miles north of Uka Kamchatka (Russia). Total distance travelled = 19,860 miles.

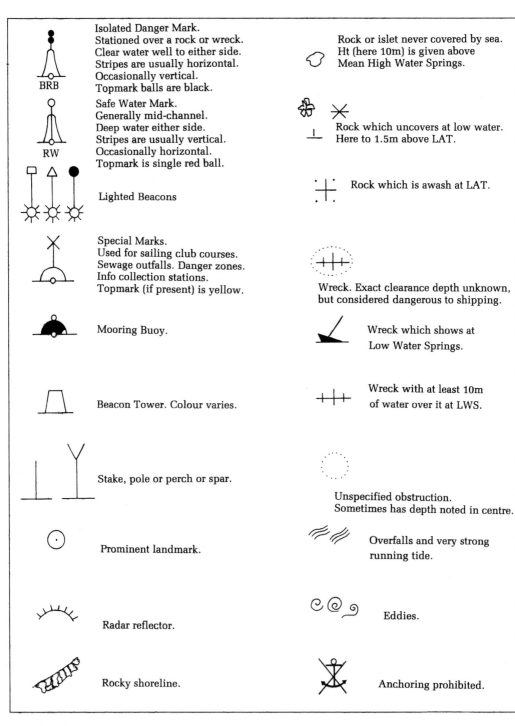

Isolated Danger Mark.
Stationed over a rock or wreck.
Clear water well to either side.
Stripes are usually horizontal.
Occasionally vertical.
Topmark balls are black.

BRB

Safe Water Mark.
Generally mid-channel.
Deep water either side.
Stripes are usually vertical.
Occasionally horizontal.
Topmark is single red ball.

RW

Lighted Beacons

Special Marks.
Used for sailing club courses.
Sewage outfalls. Danger zones.
Info collection stations.
Topmark (if present) is yellow.

Mooring Buoy.

Beacon Tower. Colour varies.

Stake, pole or perch or spar.

Prominent landmark.

Radar reflector.

Rocky shoreline.

Rock or islet never covered by sea.
Ht (here 10m) is given above
Mean High Water Springs.

Rock which uncovers at low water.
Here to 1.5m above LAT.

Rock which is awash at LAT.

Wreck. Exact clearance depth unknown,
but considered dangerous to shipping.

Wreck which shows at
Low Water Springs.

Wreck with at least 10m
of water over it at LWS.

Unspecified obstruction.
Sometimes has depth noted in centre.

Overfalls and very strong
running tide.

Eddies.

Anchoring prohibited.

Hazard marks.

3
THE MARINE CHART

The compass provides the signposts to show you your way around the roads of the sea, but you cannot use these indicators unless you know where you are in the first place and where you want to go to. In this respect, the marine chart differs from the land map because your passage is not routed and constrained by roads. On the other hand, it is similar in that you need to learn to interpret its signs and symbols – in other words, learn its language.

To use a marine chart in navigation, there are a number of things you must be able to do. These are:

1. Transfer compass bearings to and from the paper.
2. Understand the symbols, signs and abbreviations.
3. Plot a position by relating to objects in view.
4. Plot a position from digital information.
5. Measure distances.
6. Set and adjust a course for speed and safety.
7. Plan a route.
8. Understand the height, speed and direction of tides.
9. Derive a lot of pleasure from learning these skills which are quite simple and a lot of fun to do.

You have already done the first and there is plenty of help for the remainder.

Signs and Symbols

Every feature of marine life and activity has its own chart symbol. Once you can interpret these symbols you will be able to get a vast amount of detail from the several thousand marine maps published in the UK alone, but this does mean that the list of symbols is long. Not even a professional

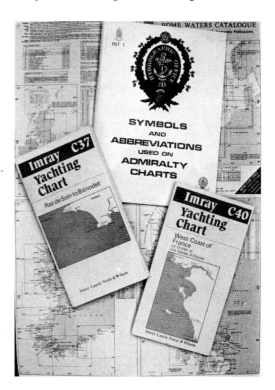

Chart conventions are given on the back of Imray charts and on Admiralty Chart 5011.

seaman will pretend to carry absolutely every chart symbol in his head. We all have to look something up from time to time, but most people soon become very familiar with the most common symbols.

The most comprehensive source of chart information is the Admiralty Chart 5011, which is not a chart at all, but a very interesting 75-page booklet describing all the notations and graphics to be found on charts produced by the Admiralty themselves, and by other organizations which produce them under licence using Admiralty information. A digest of the most important conventions will also be found on the back of many Imray charts. As you go through these and through Chart 5011, you will realize that there is a logic about chart symbols which makes them both easy to remember and to use.

Buoyage

The way in which channels and hazards are marked is a good example of this logic. The most regularly used channels are delineated by buoys and other marks which have been internationally agreed. As the vessel proceeds upstream, into a harbour, or in the direction of a normal

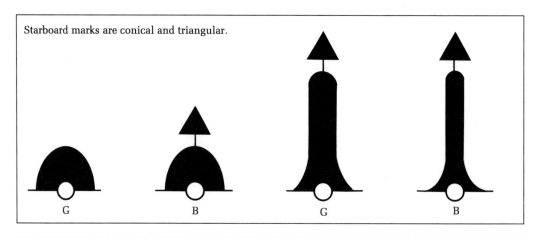

Starboard marks are conical and triangular.

G   B   G   B

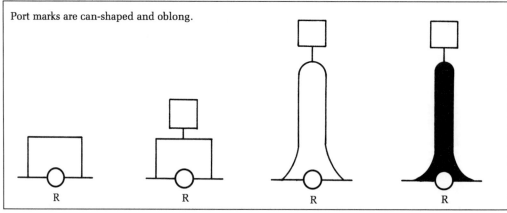

Port marks are can-shaped and oblong.

R   R   R   R

flood tide, those marks which are green are allowed to pass down the starboard side of the boat. These channel indicators, or lateral marks, will generally be cone-shaped, pointed or triangular.

The red buoys are left on the port hand. These will be flat-topped, look like baskets, be can-shaped, or cylindrical. Just like the starboard marks above, many of these buoys will be further identified by having a name painted on them, or even a serial number.

Exercise 3.1

The chart illustrated shows a narrow, twisting channel marked by lateral buoys. Imagine that you are a navigator calling instructions to a helmsman to identify each mark and how it should be passed. For example: 'Number one. Red can, leave very close to port.'

Channel indicators are called lateral marks; other sea signposts follow an agreed IALA (International Association of Lighthouse Authorities) system.

IALA Buoyage

The international system is also logical. Each mark is designated according to whether it is placed N,S,E or W of the hazard it indicates – for example, a north marker is placed N of the rock or wreck, and the skipper knows that as long as he keeps his ship to the north of the buoy he will be in deep water.

Each buoy consists of:

1. A distinctively shaped topmark.
2. A colour pattern.
3. A flashing light sequence.

We all have our own ways of memorizing these important safety and navigation aids. My own are fairly common and are detailed below:

Topmarks
North – two triangles on their base. 'They point up, and that indicates north to me.'
South – two triangles on their points. 'They point down, and that indicates south to me.'
East – two triangles base to base. 'They

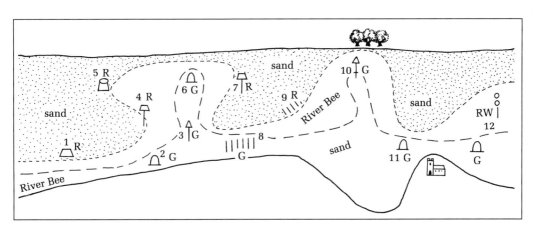

Chart for Exercise 3.1.

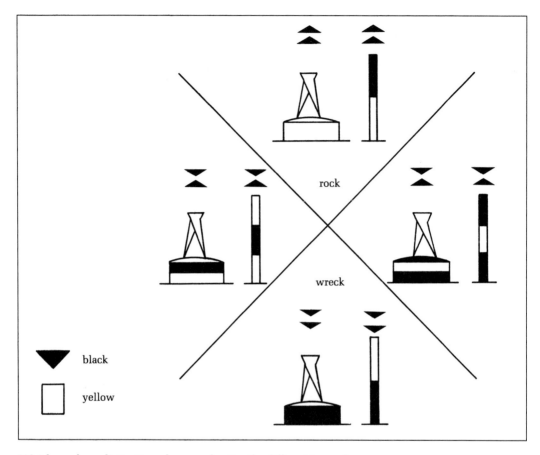

IALA buoys have distinctive colours, and notice the different topmarks.

make a diamond and diamonds come from the East.'

West – two triangles point to point. 'It is different from the other easy three and looks like 2 Vs, or a W for West.' (If you are acquainted with a foreign language, the letter W is often pronounced 'double V'.)

Colours

(Always read these from top to bottom.)
North – black/yellow. 'Just remember black over yellow.'
South – yellow/black. 'Yellow over black is the opposite of north.'

East – black/yellow/black. East is next round the clock from north and starts with the same first colour.'
West – yellow/black/yellow. 'The odd one out. West is next to south and starts with the same top colour.'

Lights

North – quick, continuous flashing.
East – three flashes.
South – six flashes.
West – nine flashes.
From north, the flash count goes up in threes and follows the clock face.

THE MARINE CHART

Exercise 3.2

You are able to recognize one feature of each of the marks leading you towards an unknown harbour. Which side of each will you pass?

1. *E.
2. Qk Fl (6).
3. BY.
4. *S.
5. Qk F.
6. YBY.
7. Qk Fl (9).
8. YB.
9. *N.
10. BYB.

Exercise 3.3

Write down the requested characteristics of the cardinal marks 1–10 below. For example, E topmark = two triangles base to base.

1. W colour.
2. N topmark.
3. S light.
4. E colour.
5. S colour.
6. W topmark.
7. E light.
8. N colour.
9. W light.
10. S topmark.

Plotting with Objects in View

Not knowing where you are is the worst of all seagoing sensations because you always fear that you are going to hit something. As the saying goes, 'It is not the sea the sailor fears, but the land.' A good navigator identifies his position constantly and marks it on the chart.

The simplest way to identify your position is with a hand-bearing compass

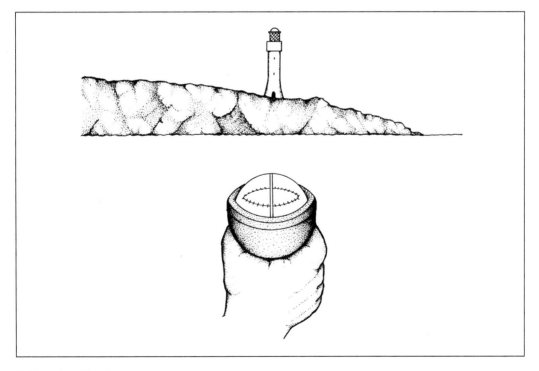

Taking a hand bearing.

25

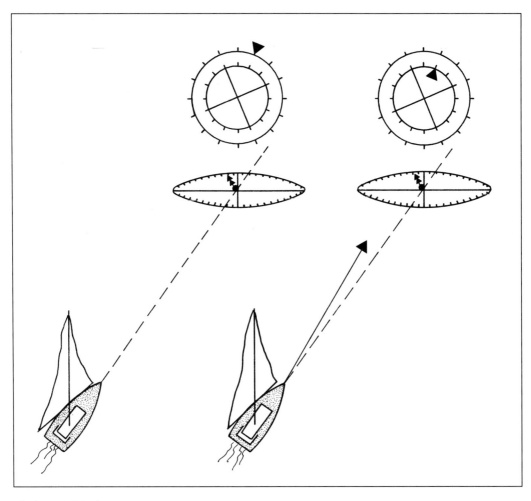

The buoy is NE of you.

on an identified object which is both in view and on the chart – for example, buoy, lighthouse, rock, headland, church, water tower or river mouth. Basically, the compass tells you that a buoy is at 045° (NE) from you, and that shows you that you are in safe water (*see* chartlet). If you use the parallel rules or a Breton plotter to draw a line on the reciprocal of 045 (045 + 200 = 245 – 20 = 225), your position must be somewhere along that line.

If you then turned the boat and headed straight towards the church and observed that it was exactly N of you, this would enable you to draw in a second reciprocal line, taken by drawing a parallel of the N–S grid on the chart. Your position is where the two lines cross. If you are a 'belt and braces' person, you could check this out with a third compass bearing on the pylon E of you. You will then be thinking like a careful navigator. Check your position three times and put a mark on the chart just once.

The symbol for an estimated position worked out by timing, looking around and so on is a dot inside a triangle, with the time written alongside – △12.15. If you are very sure of the position, the plotted position is marked with a dot inside a circle and the time again noted alongside – ⊙ 09.30.

Exercise 3.4

You are the yacht in the circle. Using the chart opposite, what approximate courses would you steer to go to:

1. The anchorage at A?
2. The quay at B?
3. The river entrance at C?
4. The mooring buoy at D?
5. What colours and light sequences would you expect to see at E?

Plotting from Digital Information

Fixing a position from a given latitude and longitude, or translating a position into that code, is no more difficult than using the grid system of an Ordnance Survey map. A modern boat will derive much of its positional information from Decca, GPS or Loran-C receivers on board. This information comes as two sets of figures which must be interpreted as a spot on the chart. Alternatively, you will often wish to put a position into a navigation machine, to work everything back the other way.

Latitude and Longitude

The circles drawn around a globe (like the equator and the tropic of Capricorn) are called the parallels of latitude because they are actually parallel to each other for the whole of the circumference. The

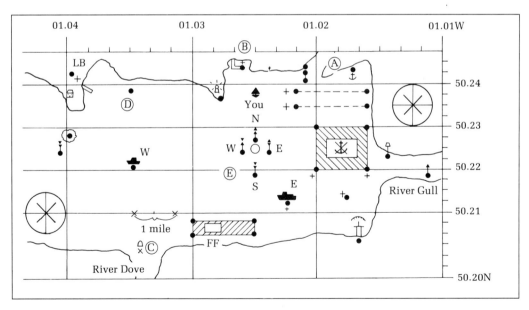

Chart for Exercises 3.4.

Digital information is very clear.

A typical Decca receiver.

A typical GPS display . . .

. . . can also have a plotter tracing the boat's course.

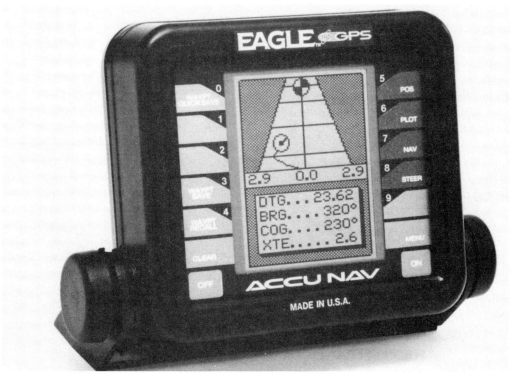

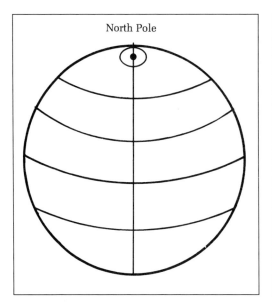

Parallels of latitude.

Meridians of longitude.

distances between them and any inter-mediate spaces are measured at either side of the chart.

The vertical lines converge at the poles, so they are not parallel to each other and are called meridians of longitude. The Greenwich meridian is the best example, being of longitude zero and measured at the top and bottom of the chart. Places are said to be east of Greenwich (for example, Paris) or west of it (for example, Land's End).

To be able to use the system of latitude and longitude in navigation, we need to have some idea of how it works. The system is called 'angular distance'. We have already learned that each degree can be divided into sixty minutes, and this fact will be used in the brief explanation below. The explanation refers to latitude, but longitude works on roughly the same principles.

Angular Distance

Imagine the earth as a complete sphere with a free-swinging metal bar on a pivot at its very centre and stretching out to touch the circumference at the earth's crust on the equator. If you move this bar through a horizontal circle it will trace the line of the equator, whilst raising it through a right angle will cause it to show on the surface at the North Pole.

Let us raise our bar by 1°. We have now travelled 60 nautical miles north of the equator. By raising it another degree, our day's run has become 120 nautical miles – a reasonable 24-hour passage for a small sailing cruiser. If 1 degree equals 60 nautical miles, it follows that 1 minute (which we know to be one-sixtieth of a degree) must correlate to 1 nautical mile. Because we are on a curved surface and marking off our distance by altering the angle of our theoretical bar, we can say:

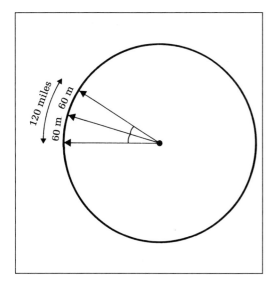

An angle becomes a distance in nautical miles.

60 nautical miles = 1 degree of arc, written as 01°

1 nautical mile = 1 minute of arc, written as 01′

A position 135 nautical miles N of the equator can therefore be shown as 02°15′00N – in other words, 2 degrees plus an extra 15 minutes north.

With the precision of satellite navigation we can occasionally even work in seconds of a degree. This is rarely the province of the leisure boat navigator, because it correlates to about 2m (7ft), but this degree of accuracy is often used by surveyors charting wrecks or positioning oil-drilling pipes.

Notice that the term nautical mile is used repeatedly here. This is a very precise geographical distance of 6,080ft and should not be confused with the statutory mile (5,280ft) which Queen Elizabeth I

arbitrarily decreed should 'be equal to 8 furlongs of 40 perches of 16½ feet each'. The sea mile or nautical mile is abbreviated to nm – usually, but not always, written in lower case letters.

For simplicity's sake, let us assume for the moment that a pivot suspended from the North Pole and sweeping the equator would give degrees and minutes east and west of Greenwich (longitude) on exactly the same principle as our pivoted bar.

Ancient and Modern

Ancient mariners used to work everything in degrees, minutes and seconds, but we moderns are constrained by computers, which prefer to handle small distances in decimal notation. General practice today is therefore to divide the separate miles into tenths and hundredths – in other words, to two decimal places.

So, a position 180 nautical miles north of the equator and 5 degrees west of Greenwich could be written as:

03°00.00N 05°00.00W

Below are some other examples of distances north of the equator and east or west of Greenwich:

125nm and 5.5°W – 02°05′00N 05°05′00W.
300nm and 6.25°W – 05°00′00N 06°25′00W.
315.5nm and 1.75°W – 05°15′50N 01°75′00E.

All this information is printed clearly along the sides, top and bottom of all charts.

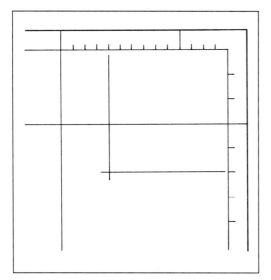

Latitude is marked on the edge of a chart and longitude is marked along the top.

aligns with a transverse line on the chart, slide it up to your latitude figure (or across to your longitude figure) and draw a small line roughly where your position should be.

The roller ruler (*see* illustration on page 11) is also a very useful navigation device and is a super, rapid way of transferring lines to a parallel position either across or up and down the chart. It is quite simple to use, exactly as the illustration shows.

A pair of dividers can also be used to measure up or down from any printed, whole number on the chart edge coinciding with a latitude line across the chart. Keep the dividers as they are and move them out to your approximate position and make a mark. Repeat the operation for longitude and insert a short,

Putting Positions on the Chart

Latitude is always taken from the edge of the chart, roughly opposite the position in question. It is measured along the chart's very precise East–West line, at right angles to the upright and parallel to the matrix lines of latitude running across the chart. Longitude is measured from the top and bottom edges of the chart, precisely along the North–South line, at right angles to the horizontal border and parallel with the vertical meridian lines drawn on the chart.

Where a line of latitude and longitude cross each other, we have an identifiable and describable position. You can transfer the edge information to the centre of the chart by three methods.

Using the parallel rule is the simplest method, as long as you ensure that it

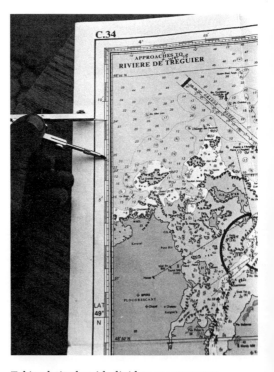

Taking latitude with dividers or compasses.

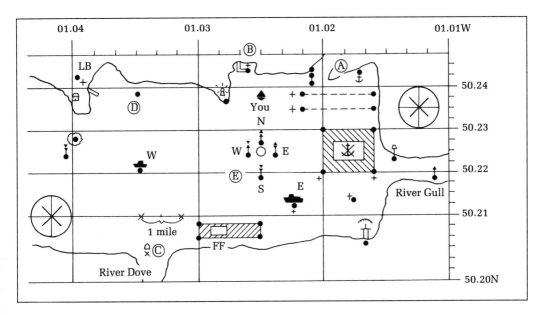

Chart for Exercises 3.5, 3.6, 3.7, 3.8 and 3.9.

lightly drawn line where the point is placed. This method needs more care, but is probably the quickest of the three. Many navigators use it when they are just getting an approximate position on the chart, without wishing to write it in with a symbol and the time. The exact position is where the two short, faint lines cross. To translate a waypoint or a buoy from chart to figures, reverse the process. The key to accuracy is the maintenance of parallelism.

Exercise 3.5

Referring to the chart above, what will you find at the approximate positions below.

Note To improve observation and chart familiarity the gradations of the latitude scale on the chart are different for some minutes of arc. This would not be so on a commercial chart.

1. 50.24.10N 01.01.80W.
2. 50.23.60N 01.02.87W.
3. 50.24.05N 01.02.03W.
4. 50.21.95N 01.02.60W.
5. 50.22.00N 01.03.50W.
6. 50.22.50N 01.02.50W.
7. 50.22.55N 01.02.40W.
8. 50.21.90N 01.01.15W.
9. 50.22.90N 01.03.97W.
10. 50.20.75N 01.01.75W.

Exercise 3.6

Referring to the chart above, give the approximate lat./long. co-ordinates for the following:

1. The RNLI station.
2. The F R harbour light.
3. Yacht travelling W.
4. Buoy marking NW end of ski zone.
5. Buoy marking SE limit of anchorage-prohibited area.

6. The S mark guarding the wreck.
7. Ship steaming E.
8. Centre of measured mile.
9. NE limit of fish farm.
10. Fairway buoy of River Dove.

Exercise 3.7

Referring to the chart on page 33, open your dividers to the following measurements. What approximate distance do they cover?

1. 2cm.   4. 10.5cm.
2. 5cm.   5. 5.5cm.
3. 3cm.

Exercise 3.8

Referring to the chart on page 33, approximately how far is it from:

1. Measured mile to ship going W?
2. W to E of fish farm?
3. N to S of anchorage prohibited area?
4. River Dove to River Gull?
5. Ship going E to ship going W?

Exercise 3.9

Referring to the chart on page 33, plot the approximate course and distance between:

1. River Dove fairway buoy to ship going W.
2. N cardinal to anchorage.
3. Ship going E to submerged rock.
4. Lighthouse to yacht.
5. River Gull starboard mark to harbour light.

Measuring Nautical Miles

In addition to showing position co-ordinates, the latitude scale is also used for the measurement of distance – remember that 1 minute of arc is one-sixtieth of a degree and equals 1 nautical mile. Measuring distance is very much easier than any of the chartwork done up to this point. One large division on our chart is equal to 1 nautical mile.

Fractions of a mile are measured from the smaller marks in each section. These vary from chart to chart, but are normally plotted in quarters, or in tenths. Both of these intermediate divisions have their best uses at different times. Any distances in between are estimated, but once we get down to this small scale, the distances will not be great so small discrepancies between one skipper's estimate and another can be ignored.

Route Planning and Course Laying

You now have sufficient skills to plan a short trip in coastal waters, so let us go on a cruise (*see* the chart opposite).

We shall leave our berth at Mudhaven and 'eyeball' our way down the River Bee to its entrance (indicated by a red and white safe-water mark). Before slipping, we shall calculate the lat./long. of this position and all the other significant marks and turning points along the way, because later on we shall be using them as input for an electronic navigation system. Just now, though, we shall take them for practice.

Our cruise takes us from Bee Fairway to pick up a passenger from Sandhole Jetty, and then on through the gap between

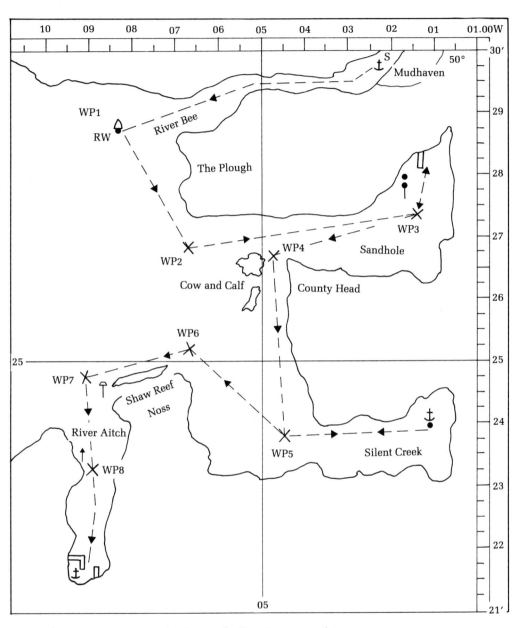

Passage from River Bee to River Aitch – use for Exercises 3.10 and 3.11.

County Head and the Cow and Calf rocks to anchor for a picnic in Silent Creek. After lunch, we shall round the Noss and Shaw Reef, and go up the River Aitch to anchor just west of the fish quay in Sandy Harbour.

As for every sea journey, we begin by marking off on the chart the safe places to pass rocks and headlands and where the deep water will be in channels. When we have joined them together, we have a route which will avoid hazards and keep us in deep water.

Exercise 3.10

Using the chart on page 35, make a note of the approximate latitude and longitude of each waypoint and turning point from Bee Fairway to the final anchorage. Include both the start and finish point:

1.	S.	6.	WP5.
2.	WP1.	7.	WP6.
3.	WP2.	8.	WP7.
4.	WP3.	9.	WP8.
5.	WP4.	10.	F.

Exercise 3.11

Using the chart on page 35, estimate the approximate course and distance between each of the waypoints. Do this by eye for course and by using your fingers for approximate distance:

1.	S–WP1.	6.	WP5–WP6.
2.	WP1–WP2.	7.	WP6–WP7.
3.	WP2–WP3.	8.	WP7–WP8.
4.	WP3–WP4.	9.	WP8–F.
5.	WP4–WP5.		

Speed and Time of Arrival

Speed, time and distance are the mathematical trinity of all cruising. However, perhaps mathematical is too grand a word for what really only amounts to simple arithmetic. I mostly do the sums in my head or on a scrap of paper, unless the numbers are inconvenient when I resort to a pocket calculator.

Speed can be obtained from the boat's log or, increasingly these days, from the satellite navigator. If you know the distance between two points and the time it took you to cover it, you can soon calculate your boat speed.

More usually, however, skippers assume that they can make a certain speed and are more interested instead in their estimated time of arrival (ETA). This is especially important in tidal rivers, or at marinas with limited lock gate opening times, where to arrive too late can mean not getting into a safe berth for the night.

Below are listed a number of formulae to help you make your assessments. We all have slight variations on these, so do not feel 'unseamanlike' if you amend them to suit your own way of working. All the workings are to the following units: speed in knots; distance in nautical miles; time in minutes.

To calculate boat speed

$$\text{Speed} = \frac{\text{distance} \times 60}{\text{time}}$$

To calculate time of arrival

$$\text{Time} = \frac{\text{distance} \times 60}{\text{speed}}$$

To calculate distance run (or to run)

$$\text{Distance} = \frac{\text{Speed} \times \text{Time}}{60}$$

Exercise 3.12

Assuming there is still water and no wind, if your boat speed is 5 knots, work out how long each of the following legs will take you.

1. 10nm.
2. 01nm.
3. 08nm.
4. 0.75nm.
5. 134nm.
6. 67nm.
7. 33nm.
8. 06nm.
9. 47nm.
10. 12.5nm.

Exercise 3.13

Below are further examples of speed, distance and time calculations, this time to be worked on the calculator.

Note T = time (in hours); D = distance (in nautical miles); S = speed (in knots).

1. 2.3 hours @ 4.7kn.
2. 12.5nm in 1.5 hours.
3. 1.5 hours for 3.75nm.
4. 135nm @ 4.6kn.
5. 6.75 hours @ 12.75kn
6. 20nm in 3.75 hours.
7. 2nm in 3 hours.
8. 18 hours for 82nm.
9. 75nm in 12.5 hours.
10. From 50.43.00N on course 180T to 50.20.00N in 4 hours.

The Beaufort Scale		
Strength	State	Speed (knots)
0	Calm	0–1
1	Light air	1–3
2	Light breeze	4–6
3	Gentle breeze	7–10
4	Moderate breeze	11–16
5	Fresh breeze	17–21
6	Strong breeze	22–27
7	Near gale	28–33
8	Gale	34–40
9	Severe gale	41–47
10	Storm	48–55
11	Violent storm	56–63
12	Hurricane	64+

The Wave Scale		
Code	Sea state	Wave height (ft)
0	Glassy	0
1	Ripples	0–1
2	Wavelets	1–2
3	Slight	2–4
4	Moderate	4–8
5	Rough	8–13
6	Very rough	13–20
7	High	20–30
8	Very high	30–45
9	Phenomenal	45+

4

MORE ABOUT THE CHART

Because the aim of this book is to keep things simple we will not fall into the traps of boredom and complexity which seem so beloved of the marine trade tuition and examination industry. Some testers delight in throwing in questions about very unusual marks or unusual lights, almost as though they expect the student to know them all. A well-equipped boat would have a number of quick-reference cards readily to hand (*see* photograph below), so a skipper seeing something

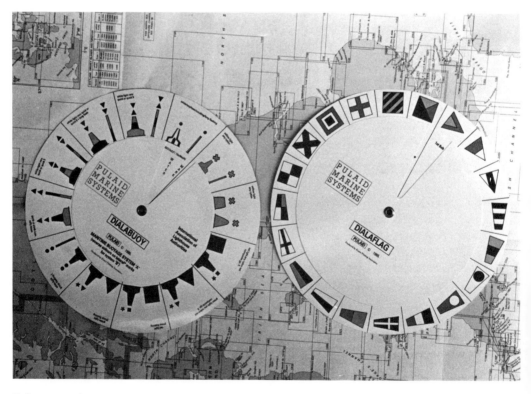

Reference cards.

which he or she does not recognize can very soon look it up.

Having said that, there are a number of navigation and boat management tasks which crop up very regularly, so the chart symbols and conventions concerned automatically commit themselves to memory. However, in order to get ourselves started, it is not a bad plan to try to commit the most important symbols to memory.

The best way to learn about charts is to study them. Even though I spend about five months a year at sea, I still regularly get out the charts during my closed season, and use them to enjoy imaginary voyages and to have the fun of planning entrances to strange harbours. This experience has coloured the nature of the information set out below, which is a potpourri of the chart notations which I use most often. The exercises which follow are also typical of the sort of navigational task which cruising skippers perform all day and every day.

The data arranges itself into four main categories: buoys; hazards; depth contours; lights and beacons. Also, note that in the drawings I have used conventional international abbreviations and codings. You will meet these very often in your life afloat, so they are listed at the head of each appropriate section.

Buoys

In addition to the cardinal marks and channel signposts already discussed, you should have instant recall of several other buoys, either when you see them on the chart or when you are spotting them from the boat.

Colour Codings

W = white; R = red; G = green;
Bu = blue; Vi = violet;
Y = yellow/orange/amber; Or = orange;
Am = amber; B = black.

Buoyage Symbols

Bn = beacon; Mk = mark; Tr = tower;
Fs = flagstaff; Ho = house;
PA = position approximate; Rk = rock.

Hazards

 Isolated danger mark – stationed over a rock or wreck with clear water well to either side. Stripes are usually horizontal, although occasionally vertical. Topmark balls are black.

 Safe-water mark – generally mid-channel with deep water to either side. Stripes are usually vertical, but occasionally horizontal. Topmark is a single red ball.

 Lighted beacons.

 Special marks – used for sailing club courses, sewage outfalls, danger zones and information collection stations. Topmark (if present) is yellow.

Mooring buoy.

 Beacon tower – colour varies.

Stake, pole or perch or spar.

 Prominent landmark.

 Radar reflector.

 Rocky shoreline.

 Rock or islet never covered by sea. Height (here 10m) is given above mean high water springs (MHWS).

Rock which uncovers at low water – here to 1.5m above lowest astronomical tide (LAT).

Rock which is awash at LAT.

 Wreck – exact clearance depth unknown, but considered dangerous to shipping.

 Wreck which shows at low water springs (LWS).

 Wreck with at least 10m of water over it at LWS.

 Unspecified obstruction – sometimes has depth noted in centre.

 Overfalls and very strong running tide.

 Eddies.

 Anchoring prohibited.

Depth Contours

A good idea of the depth of water expected at LAT is given by the following chart colours.

Yellow shows ground which dries out. The height to which it projects above the surface is indicated by an underlined figure – for example, 5.2 – showing metres and tenths of a metre. White indicates a predicted depth of less than 5m. Spot soundings are shown in metres and fractions. The figures are not

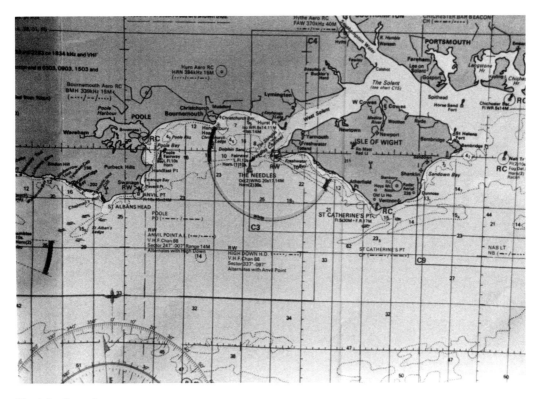

Chart depth contours.

underlined – for example, 3_1 indicates 3.1m. Blue is the colour for depths over 5m and the spot soundings are shown as whole numbers.

These depth regions are separated on the chart by a dotted line, so it is possible to navigate 'along the 5m contour'. Some passage-making charts trace contours at 10m and 20m with these depths shown at several breaks in the dotted line.

Lights and Beacons

Lt = light; F = fixed; Occ = occulting (periods of light are longer than periods of darkness); Iso = isophase (periods of light and darkness are equal); Fl = flashing (periods of darkness are longer than periods of light); Q = quick; IQ = interrupted quick; VQ = very quick (usually 100–120 flashes per minute); Al = alternating (for example, Al WR); Dir = directional; Occas = occasional; Gp = group (for example, 2 + 3 = 2 flashes, pause, 3 flashes); W = white (not always shown, if no symbol then assume white).

Many skippers enjoy being out at night because position fixing by lighthouse and lighted beacon bearings is very unambiguous. They are all different and recognizable by separate characteristics printed on the chart. As an example, here is one from the Imray C10 passage-making chart. It is the light at Normandy's Pointe de Barfleur:

Fl(2)W 10s 72m 29M

Individually, the four indicators mean:

Fl (2) This is the light's class or character. Here it shows that the flashes are in groups of two.
W The colour. There may be more than one colour, with the separate hues showing from different directions.
10s This is the light's period, or the time taken for the sequence. Here it takes 10 seconds from the start of the first flash to the start of the first flash when it repeats.
72m The elevation of the actual lamp (usually) above mean high water springs. Notice the convention that metres are always abbreviated to m in the lower case.
20M The range of Pointe de Barfleur Lighthouse is 29 nautical miles, taking no account of the curvature of the earth and assuming clear visibility. In meteorological terms, 'clear' means that you can see 10 miles. Notice the convention that nautical miles are abbreviated to M in the upper case.

Below is another example, this time for Portland Bill Lighthouse:

Fl(4) 20s 43m 29M + FR 19m 13M

This indicates that there are two lights. The principal light consists of four white flashes which take 20 seconds from start to start, and it shines from a tower which is 43m above sea level with a range of 29 nautical miles. Below this, there is a fixed red light at a height of 19m and with a range of only 13 nautical miles. On the

chart covering Portland Bill, this red section is shown to cover some rocks called The Shambles. The skipper knows that if he sees red, there are rocks between him and the light (*see* the illustration opposite).

At sea, the normal process in identifying a lighthouse is to the character (number of flashes), and then start the stopwatch.

Exercise 4.1

What will you tell your skipper about the lights below?

1. Berry Head Fl(2) 15s 58m 18M.
2. Start Point Fl(3) 10s 25m + FR 12M.
3. Les Hanois Q(2) 5s 23M.
4. La Corbière Iso WR 10s 18m 16M.
5. Portsall VQ(9) 10s 9m 8M ***

Exercise 4.2

What do the following chart abbreviations tell you?

1.	Lt.	6.	Tr.
2.	Bu.	7.	Y.
3.	BRB.	8.	Iso.
4.	Al.	9.	Fs.
5.	Bn.	10.	PA.

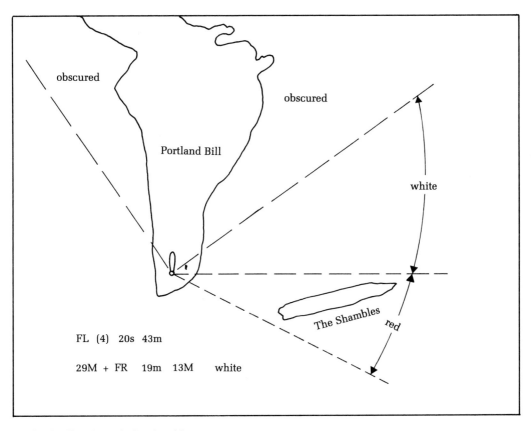

obscured

obscured

Portland Bill

white

The Shambles red

FL (4) 20s 43m

29M + FR 19m 13M white

Portland Bill Light and The Shambles.

**The Seven Watches kept by
Crews at Sea**

1200–1600 Afternoon watch
1600–1800 First dogwatch
1800–2000 Second dogwatch
2000–2400 Evening watch
2400–0400 Middle watch
0400–0800 Morning watch
0800–1200 Forenoon watch

The shorter dogwatches are inserted
to vary the hours so that no 'watch'
always has the less popular middle
and morning watches.

5

HIGH WATER AND LOW WATER

Tides concern the boat navigator in two ways:

1. They either assist or retard his forward progress, or they push him sideways. With a diagonal current flow, they can do both of these things at the same time.
2. High tides make it simple to get up rivers and to come alongside the wall in certain harbours. Low tides can make both these manoeuvres impossible. 'How much water will there be?' is a very common question on most boats.

Tidal Flow

Tidal shift is caused by the gravitational (pulling) effects of the sun and the moon. When these two bodies are in a straight line with each other, we experience large, or spring tides. When they are at right angles to each other the tides are small, or neap tides. The rise, fall and speed of flow between these extremities is proportional.

As the earth rotates, the water in its seas is being constantly sucked towards the strongest pulling body. This causes water to run out of estuaries and to be pulled along the coasts. When a part of the sea reaches a point on the earth's rotation where it is shaded or protected from the

attraction, the water is no longer pulled, so it flows back again.

Generally speaking, tides around the UK follow the directional pattern given in the illustration below. This is important because buoyage follows the direction of a flooding tide – in other words, starboard hand markers assume that the boat is travelling up the estuary.

There are a number of places from which you can obtain information about the direction and speed of the tide's flow at any given time. The most common are:

1. Tidal diamonds printed at significant places on Admiralty charts and related to an information box in the chart's corner. The speed is given in knots and the direction in degrees true.
2. Chartlets on Imray charts and those also published in such annuals as *Reed's Nautical Almanac* and *Macmillan and Silk Cut Almanac*. These show the direction as an arrow and quote average speeds for spring and neap tides.
3. The Admiralty Tide Tables.
4. Various computer programs, both for full machines and for pocket computers.

Charts are said to be reduced to Lowest Astronomical Tide (LAT), meaning that the depth shown on the chart is that level of

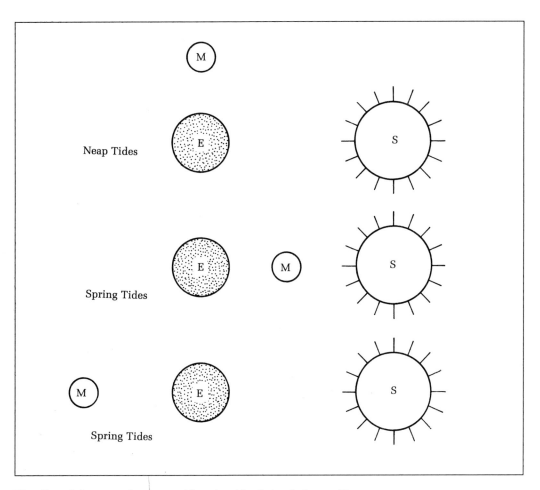

The effect of the sun and moon on tides caused by their relative positions.

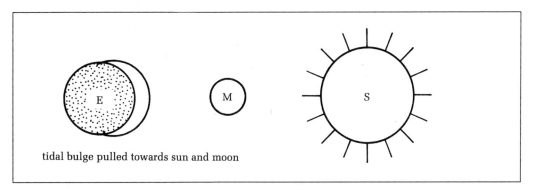

The tidal bulge on the earth.

Tides flow into estuaries.

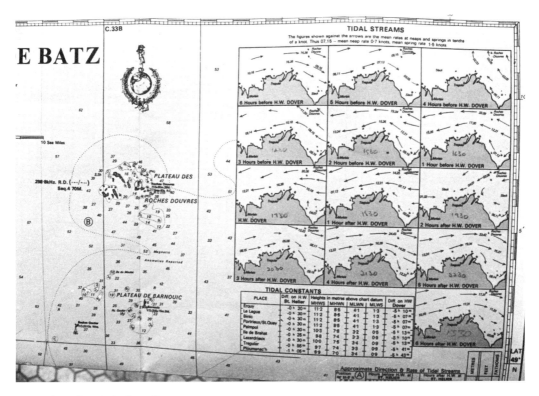

Imray charts have tide flow diagrams.

My own computer calculates tidal heights.

water which will still be present at the time of low water during the lowest tide which has been recorded. Put another way, there will always be at least the stated depth of water over a rock, or a wreck. Charts also show how high above LAT rocks and sandbanks will be if they dry out.

In between spring and neap tides, the navigator thinks of tidal height and flow as being proportional. You will also find 'mean' (or average) heights and speeds quoted for both spring and neap tides. Navigators also assume that the rise and fall will be even throughout the tide's six-hour duration. This is not always strictly accurate, but the errors are small enough to be ignored.

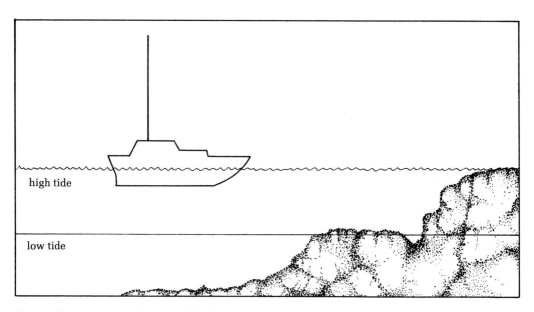

You need to have a mental picture of depth at any time.

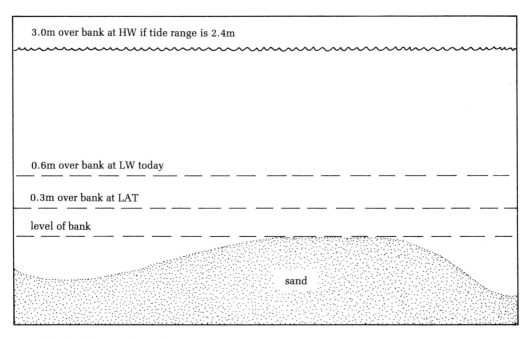

3.0m over bank at HW if tide range is 2.4m

0.6m over bank at LW today

0.3m over bank at LAT

level of bank

sand

A sandbank with a sounding of 0.5m.

The difference between low water (LW) and high water (HW) on any day is said to be the tidal range. Nowadays, it is always quoted in metres. The sources of information for any places are the same as those noted above, plus local tide table booklets.

Exercise 5.1

From table 1 below, calculate the a.m. and p.m. tidal ranges for each of the five days. What is the approximate mean range for each day?

In the sample tide table 1, the height must be added to LAT – in other words, at low water there will be a depth equivalent to the figure shown on the chart, plus the depth of water quoted in the table. Here is another example, using the chart below.

High water at 12.00 – 5.0m.
Low water at 18.00 – 1.5m.
Range is therefore 3.5m.

The chart shows the sounding on a sandbank as 0.5m. At low water it will therefore be covered to a total depth of 2.0m, and at high water the total depth will be 5.5m.

Exercise 5.2

Using the tide tables below work out approximately how much water there will be in the harbour entrance at the time given. On the chart the entrance depth is shown as 0.75m.

1.	09.00.	6.	21.00.
2.	09.30.	7.	16.00.
3.	05.00.	8.	11.00.
4.	08.00.	9.	15.00.
5.	08.30.	10.	15.00.

Day One	Day Two	Day Three	Day Four	Day Five
02.20 – 3.3m	03.10 – 3.2m	05.16 – 2.7m	01.20 – 6.9m	02.30 – 2.4m
08.50 – 0.7m	09.30 – 0.8m	11.15 – 7.1m	08.10 – 3.0m	08.20 – 6.9m
15.50 – 2.9m	15.45 – 2.9m	17.50 – 2.9m	14.30 – 6.8m	15.10 – 2.3m
21.40 – 1.0m	21.40 – 1.0m	23.40 – 7.0m	20.55 – 3.1m	20.40 – 7.2m

Table 1.

Day One	Day Two	Day Three	Day Four	Day Five
02.20 – 3.5m	03.10 – 3.3m	05.16 – 2.3m	01.20 – 6.5m	02.30 – 2.2m
08.50 – 0.6m	09.30 – 0.5m	11.15 – 7.3m	08.10 – 3.4m	08.20 – 6.7m
15.50 – 2.4m	15.45 – 2.7m	17.50 – 2.6m	14.30 – 6.3m	15.10 – 2.4m
21.40 – 1.3m	21.40 – 1.2m	23.40 – 7.4m	20.55 – 3.4m	20.40 – 7.7m

Table 2.

Low water	Hour	1	2	3	4	5	6	High water
	Rise	$\frac{1}{12}$	$\frac{2}{12}$	$\frac{3}{12}$	$\frac{3}{12}$	$\frac{2}{12}$	$\frac{1}{12}$	
	Rise	0.08	0.17	0.25	0.25	0.17	0.08	

Table 3.

The Rule of Twelfths

Many skippers use the so-called Rule of Twelfths to calculate the tide's rise and fall, and to work out the depth that can be expected at a certain place at a particular time. The Rule is not as precise as other methods which use complicated tidal curve diagrams, but the tide is itself subject to inconsistencies, so this rule of thumb works well in practice. It is certainly the method which I use ninety-nine per cent of the time on my cruising.

The Rule of Twelfths assumes that the tide rises (or falls) $\frac{1}{12}$ of its range in the first hour of the flood, $\frac{2}{12}$ in the second hour and so on as shown in the table above. The lower line gives the equivalent fractions in decimal.

Let us look at a practical example, again using an imaginary harbour (see illustration below). This shows 0.3m LAT at the entrance. The tide for today is: LW at 01.14 – 0.2m; HW at 07.55 – 5.3m; LW at

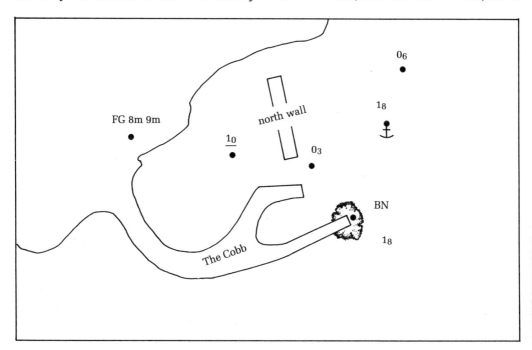

Harbour with 0.3m depth at its entrance at LAT.

Time	14.00	15.40	16.40	17.40	18.40	19.40
Lat.	0.2	0.2	0.2	0.2	0.2	0.2
Rise	0.4	0.85	1.25	1.25	0.85	0.4
Depth	0.6	1.45	2.7	3.95	4.8	5.2

Table 4.

13.39 – 0.1m; HW at 20.22 –5.0m. The Mean range is therefore 5.0m. (Note that there is no virtue in making the arithmetic too complicated, even if you are using a pocket calculator. You can round the times off to 01.15; 08.00; 13.40 and 20.20.)

Using the Rule of Twelfths table (*see* table 3), we know that if we approach the harbour during the afternoon, we shall have the depths as given in table 4 above.

If your boat draws 1.50m, you will therefore be able to get alongside the harbour at around 4 p.m.

Exercise 5.3

Using the same harbour (*see* chart on page 50), draw up the depth tables for 10.30, 11.30, 12.30, 13.30, 14.30, 15.30 and 16.30 on Tuesday 10, and 12.30, 13.30, 14.30, 15.30, 16.30, 17.30 and 18.30 on Tuesday 17 from the tidal information given.

Tue 10	Tue 17
04.17 – 4.7m	00.15 – 1.0m
10.30 – 1.3m	06.30 – 5.1m
16.44 – 5.1m	12.30 – 1.0m
22.55 – 1.0m	18.45 – 5.3m

Exercise 5.4

Your boat draws 1.5m. At what a.m. and p.m. times will you have enough water to get into the above harbour (*see* chart on page 50) during Days One to Five below? Allow 0.5m of water extra for safety reasons – in other words, calculate roughly when there will be 2.0m depth. An answer within 15 minutes of that quoted will suffice.

Day One (p.m.)	Day Two (p.m.)	Day Three (p.m.)	Day Four (a.m.)	Day Five (p.m.)
02.20 – 3.5m	03.10 – 3.3m	05.16 – 0.3m	01.20 – 6.5m	02.30 – 0.2m
08.50 – 0.6m	09.30 – 0.5m	11.15 – 7.3m	08.10 – 1.4m	08.20 – 8.7m
15.50 – 2.4m	15.45 – 2.7m	17.50 – 2.6m	14.30 – 6.3m	15.10 – 0.4m
21.40 – 1.3m	21.40 – 1.2m	23.40 – 7.4m	20.55 – 1.4m	20.40 – 8.7m

Table 5.

6
THE TIDE – FOR OR AGAINST?

A boat only very rarely actually travels in the exact direction in which its nose is pointing. There are a number of factors which cause cause the boat's course to have a sideways component as well as a forward component – a sailing boat drifting to leeward or making leeway is the most commonly quoted example of diagonal progress. However, even motor boats can be pushed sideways by the wind and all boats are influenced by the tide.

Let us forget about the effects of wind for a moment, and instead concentrate on tides by reminding ourselves that the sea in its ebb and flood does not actually go up and down but instead flows roughly parallel to the coast. It is necessary to qualify this simplified statement, however, because the direction of the tide is constantly changing. It passes through a circle as it makes the directional shift, say, from running down the Channel on

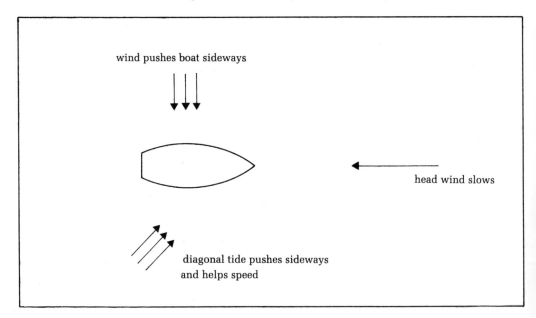

wind pushes boat sideways

head wind slows

diagonal tide pushes sideways
and helps speed

Forces acting to push the boat sideways or at a slant.

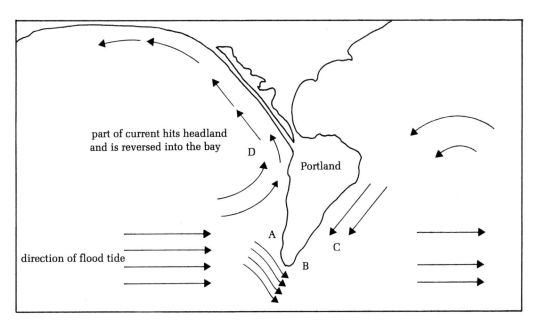

part of current hits headland
and is reversed into the bay

D

Portland

A

C

B

direction of flood tide

Portland Bill tide and counter-tide.

the ebb to coming back up again on the flood.

A headland jutting out into a tidal stream can also affect both the direction and the speed of the current. Let us look at an example – perhaps Portland Bill, or the Cotentin Peninsula jutting north from Normandy. Imagine an east-going tide hitting a headland at 2 knots. The water will be deflected, so the tide will change direction at A. The squeeze effect will send more water running around the headland at the same time, so the current will speed up appreciably at B. You would also expect some turbulence at C, where the two currents meet. A small component of the tide will be diverted the other way at D, and will give a weak stream travelling in the opposite direction and running close to the shore of a bay.

A good skipper will always be looking to use these phenomena to his or her advantage. It very often happens at sea that the quickest distance between two points is not necessarily a straight line.

Calculating Course Deviation

Depending on the direction in which you are travelling, your boat can be speeded up by the tide, slowed down by it, be pushed bodily sideways, or any combination of these effects. To keep life simple whilst we learn to cope with tidal (and estuarial) currents, let us imagine that we are in a displacement motor craft, or even a motor-sailer. The skipper of such a craft will possibly have three separate methods for working out his or her speed. These are:

1. Taking bearings as the boat passes objects along the coast, and therefore

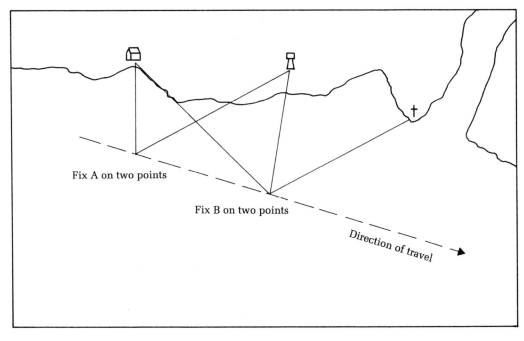

The running fix. You can establish your position and line of travel by taking compass bearings on known objects that you pass.

calculating his speed by timing each leg (*see* illustration above).

2. A well-equipped, modern boat will have its speed displayed by a Decca or a GPS unit.

3. Almost all boats have speed and distance logs worked by a small propeller, either towed behind the boat, or mounted on a transducer projecting through the hull. In its simplest form, the log impeller referred to in Point 3 above acts like a bicycle dynamo. The faster it spins, the more electrical energy it creates. This voltage either drives an analogue needle pointer, or it is converted into digital information. In still water, such a device works well, but it obviously becomes inaccurate in currents. If the boat turns into a current the exaggerated water flow speeds up the impeller, but the boat itself

slows down. Turning to run with the stream makes the boat speed up, but the impeller does not increase its speed by the same amount.

To make sure that every seafarer understands that there are big differences between the apparent speed shown by the log and the boat's actual rate of progress over the ground, there is a special technical vocabulary for the relevant terms – this vocabulary is summarized in the information box opposite.

Note that all speeds at sea are quoted in knots, one knot (1kn) being a speed equal to one nautical mile per hour (there is no such thing as knots per hour). A boat covering 6nm in an hour is said to be steaming at 6 knots. If a piece of wood is

LOG AND COMPASS TERMS

- **LSP** Log speed, sometimes also called indicated speed.
- **SOG** Actual speed over the ground (sometimes called speed made good or SMG).
- **COG/CMG** Course over the ground, or course made good.
- **XTE** Cross-track error, or the amount by which the boat moves sideways from its intended heading or the straight line from point of departure to destination (sometimes also written as CTE, or called off-track error).

carried 2nm in an hour by the current, the tide is running at two knots.

To understand the effect which tidal currents have on boats, let us subject our 5 knot motor-sailer to some actual examples. In still windless water the boat will make 5 knots. If the nose of the boat is turned directly into a 3-knot current, the SOG will drop to 2 knots (the impeller log will probably display about 7 knots). If the stern is turned to the current, this will add to the boat's speed to make 8 knots over the ground. Here the log might show about 6 knots. If the boat slants across this 3-knot tide at exactly 45°, the effect of the current will be halved. In the N–S tide of the illustration overleaf, the boat heading NE or NW will slow to 3.5 knots, but going SE or SW it will cover 6½ nautical miles every hour, or 6.5 knots.

There are tables, hand-held computer programs and arithmetic methods of working this calculation very precisely for tidal angles other than the half-cardinals, but most skippers prefer to estimate these and match the speed to accurate position fixing.

Off-Setting Course

If calculating the effect of the tidal

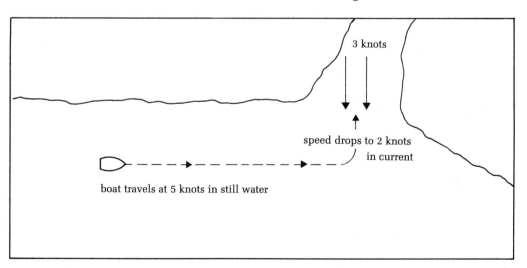

3 knots

speed drops to 2 knots
in current

boat travels at 5 knots in still water

The boat running into and with a 3kn current.

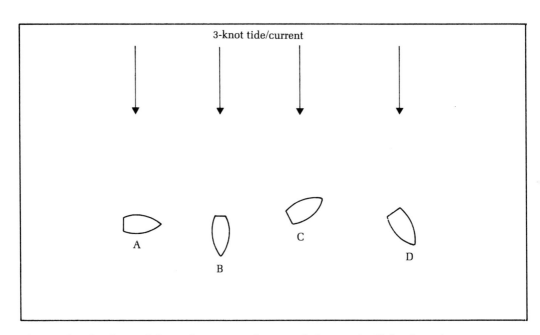

The same boat heading in different directions to show speed changes: A will do 5 knots but move sideways; B will do 8 knots; C will do 3.5 knots and slide sideways; D will do 6.5 knots and be pushed south.

currents on boat speed is not a very precise navigational science as applied in most cruising instances, we must also remember that there are occasions when an accurate course to steer (CTS) is essential. A classic and common case is when sailing a vessel from England to Cherbourg – thousands of sailors make this trip each year. Unless the yacht is well placed on the correct side of the rhumbline course over the last 10 nautical miles, it risks being swept down to Alderney or up to Calais by the strong tide. Over the final 20nm, a prudent skipper will work a very precise tidal off-set diagram. The example below is a much simplified version of this.

Tidal Off-Set Example

The yacht is travelling from Aport to Bport, a distance of 5nm (*see* the illustration opposite). Boat speed is 5 knots, CTS is 0.90T; tide is 180/1 knot (unlike wind, tide is always shown in the direction in which it is running – not from where it came as with an east wind). In the hour's passage, the yacht will be pushed 1nm south of its destination. The remedy is to steer 1nm north of it, but what course is that?

1. The method of calculating the CTS is to set the sideways drift on your dividers (here 1nm).
2. From the start point, draw a line on the chart parallel to the direction of the current (here 000/180 or N–S).
3. Step the divider distance down this line and mark it 'S' for start.
4. Join S to your destination 'D' by drawing a line from one to the other.
5. Measure this CTS from the compass rose (here it is approximately 070T).

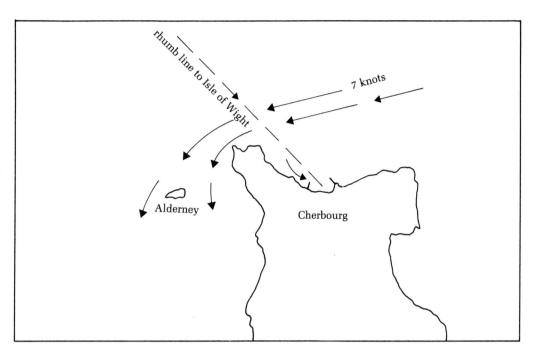

A yacht sailing from the Isle of Wight to Cherbourg may be swept to Alderney in a strong tide.

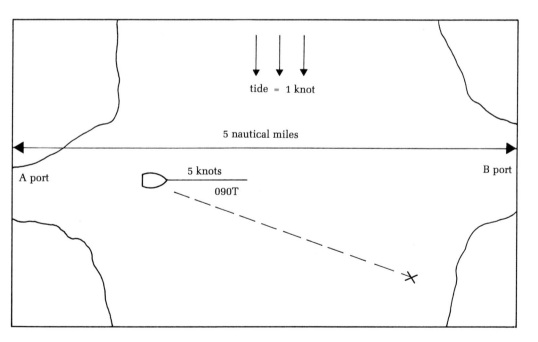

Aport to Bport.

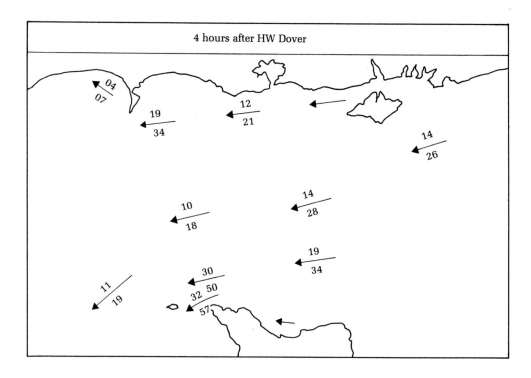

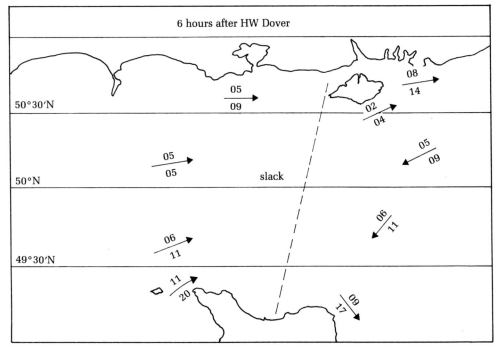

Two typical tidal flow diagrams.

Exercise 6.1

What will be the approximate CTS if the tidal speed is:

1. 0.50.   4. 2.75.
2. 1.50.   5. 3.00.
3. 2.50.

A Longer Journey

On a passage like a Channel crossing which might take up to twenty hours, the tide will change direction several times. In order to be well placed towards the end of the trip, the navigator uses tide diagrams to calculate (and estimate) how far the boat will be moved east or west during each hour of the crossing.

A simple way to do this is to plot an hourly table in two columns. The example shown in this chapter (*see* page 61) is a table used on a crossing from Lyme Regis to Cherbourg in a motor-sailer which can be relied on to plod along at an average 5 knots. The distance is 80 miles. The tidal diagrams have been made up, but they are fairly typical of the sort of material which is to be found in nautical almanacs published in Britain and in most other countries of the world.

For our purpose we will assume that high water (HW in Dover) is 17.00 and that we shall slip our berth at about noon, 5 hours before HW Dover. Look at the chartlets opposite. You should notice several things about them.

1. British tides are usually referenced to Dover and also to the nearest standard port (a location where tidal observations are maintained and for which annual tide prediction tables are published). Tides for ports in between are predicted by adding or subtracting quoted times of HW and LW (low water) from those of the standard port.

2. Times and flow rates are 'predictions'. Their absolute accuracy is not guaranteed because so many unpredictable factors can influence them. High atmospheric pressure, for example, will speed them up and increase their range. For this reason, a beginner navigator might be puzzled to see slight time and height discrepancies between one set of tables and another. These occur because all such material has to be 'guesstimated' and the estimate depends to some degree on who made it. In practice, however, this has little effect because, as I have said, nobody can predict tide to the nearest centimetre or to a precise couple of minutes.

3. The convention is to give flow rates for average neap tides (the lower figure) and for average spring tides (the higher figure, usually on the right). No decimal point is included, so 08.25 means that during an average neap tide the current will be running at just over ¾ knot, increasing to 2½ knots at spring tides.

Remember that these are median figures. The 08 rate will be less for a tide of very small range, but the 25 rate could be as much as 1 knot faster during, say, the very large equinoctial tides. If the tidal range is half-way between neaps and springs, the flow speed will also be halved (in this example, 2.5 – 0.8 = 1.7 ÷ 2 = 0.85 + 0.8⅙ knot). All other times are in direct proportion, but because the speeds are low and the distances small, intelligent estimation is perfectly adequate for most cruising skippers.

4. The arrows give an indication of direction and speed. If they are thick, long and close together, a fast current can be

expected. Admiralty charts give the flow direction in three-figure notation, but this is too precise for most skippers who tend to round them off to simpler figures. Generally speaking, the chartlets are easier to use.

5.   Notice how the tide is much less in Lyme Bay (or in any other bay for that matter) and how it gets up to 5.7 knots between the peninsula and Alderney – the infamous Alderney race.

My own 'record' on passage from Lyme Regis to Alderney was when I was carried 15 miles west of my rhumb-line course. I also reached over 12 knots in a similar tide race near Ushant. This is quite remarkable, because my boat's maximum hull speed is only 8 knots, but it does show

why a navigator needs a very sound knowledge of tides.

How to Use the Tide Chartlets

This is my own system, but it is typical of many. Experienced Channel crossers seldom fight the tide. You will have a faster crossing in a sail boat, or aboard a motor-sailer, by steering the rhumb-line but letting yourself be carried down Channel by the ebb and back up again by the flood. If you attempt to hold the rhumb line by steering 'up-tide', the boat speed may be more than halved. Even in a power cruiser, trying to hold the line when there is something like a 2–3 knot tide running is a very inefficient way of driving the boat.

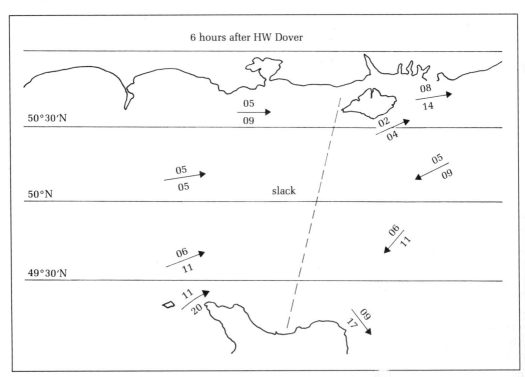

Add latitude and longitude lines to aid your estimates.

The most efficient method is as follows (*see* also the illustration opposite).

1. Make copies of the tidal diagrams on the back and front of an A4 page. You then only have one sheet at the nav station.
2. On each chartlet, draw in the latitude lines for 50.30N as a solid line, and the 50.15N and 50.45N as pecked lines. Inserting these is simple if you use compasses to prescribe small arcs from the solid lines, and then simply join their crests.
3. Draw in the rhumb line from Lyme Regis to Cherbourg.
4. Make a table showing approximately where you expect to be for each hour of the tide. You can do this simply by putting dots or small figures on the chartlet. Here, you are really inserting your estimated positions.
5. Estimate how far east or west of your rhumb line course you expect to be pushed in each hour and add these up for each tidal cycle (*see* the example in the table shown). You will then know roughly how far east or west of your target you can expect to be.

Thus, the boat will be approximately 5 nautical miles east of Cherbourg when you arrive at 07.00. This means that when the tide is running hard west from 19.00–01.00, you should ease the helm a little to make a bit more westing to compensate. You should also bear in mind the fact that this is only an estimation – a game plan – which might well be adjusted as you go along, so keep a very precise check on your position, especially over the last few hours.

On this particular route, there is plenty of help from powerful lighthouses at Portland Bill, St Catherine's Point, Cap de la Hague and Barfleur. There are also plenty of radio direction-finding beacons. However, even though I mostly navigate my boat by Decca and GPS, I still plot by these other methods and by radar bearings just to keep these skills honed for when they are needed. A navigator has much better peace of mind when he has several systems which check each other out and all agree with each other.

EXAMPLE OF COURSE DEVIATION

HW Dover	Departure Lyme Regis
17.00	12.00

TIME	WEST	EAST
12.00–13.00		0.50
13.00–14.00		0.50
14.00–15.00		0.75
15.00–16.00		0.75
16.00–17.00		0.75
17.00–18.00		0.00
18.00–19.00		0.00
19.00–20.00	0.75	
20.00–21.00	1.00	
21.00–22.00	1.25	
22.00–23.00	1.30	
23.00–00.00	0.75	
00.00–01.00	0.50	
01.00–02.00		0.50
02.00–03.00		0.75
03.00–04.00		1.25
04.00–05.00		1.50
05.00–06.00		1.75
06.00–07.00		1.50

Total   W = 5.55   E = 10.50

7
THE SHIP'S LOG

If you go aboard a strange boat and wish to check the quality of the navigation, have a look at the log book. Good navigators keep very detailed records as to where they are at any one time, as well as other information such as where the ship's head is pointing, and what the tide and the weather are doing as they write. It is not that a keen log-keeper is over-meticulous, but that he enjoys what he is doing and therefore probably does it well. That philosophy is part of the rationale of this book: what you do well you enjoy, and what you enjoy you will do well. You already have enough to start to do things well, so I hope that you are enjoying it too.

The log has four principal purposes:

A Cruising Association (CA) log.

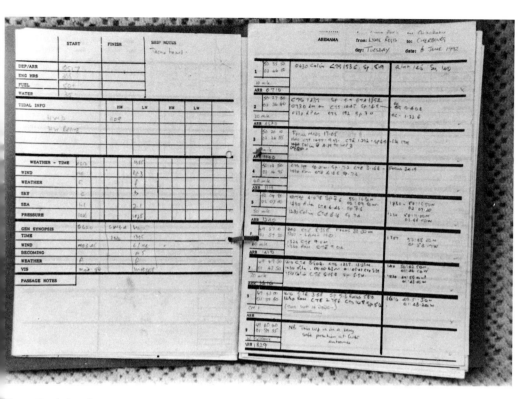

The author's log sheet.

1. It is a good record of the voyage.

2. It lets you know where you were an hour ago, so you have a reference point if other systems fail.

3. It is a good way of knowing how your boat is performing under engine, sails and so on.

4. It serves as a super way of forecasting and planning next summer's trip.

My own system has stood the test of time. It is a combination of traditional formats with some additions which I have devised to bring modern electronics into play.

The system divides into two separate halves:

1. Sheet one comes in two parts. It is a planning sheet which is filled in before you weigh anchor. It has archive information and a page for information which will be offered to the Decca and GPS navigator.

2. Sheet two is the hour-by-hour record of what is happening to the boat and its surroundings. As well as being an official document which can be demanded by various people, it is also an excellent and evocative diary of all those small happenings which time erases from the human memory.

Sheet one is a double-sided loose-leaf page which is kept on the chart table and later

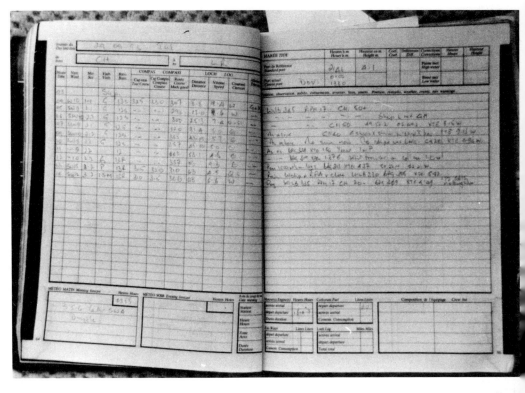

The author's passage log.

put into a file. I started off having sheet two as a spiral-bound book, but have since changed to loose-leaf pages because a single page occupies less chart table space, a fair copy can be made at the end of the journey, and it can be made double-sided to give enough space for longer passages.

Completing Sheet One

Side One

1. The first page is largely self-explanatory, but it is useful to keep a note of engine hours and other capacities.

2. The tidal information can refer to departure and arrival ports, and to Dover, which is simpler for some tide flow charts.
3. A separate, hourly or two-hourly weather synopsis is just one more aid to forecasting, especially if you believe in such useful rhymes as:
  'Sharp rise after low,
  Foretells another blow.'
4. I record the BBC Shipping Forecasts on a separate dedicated sheet (weather recording sheet). The weather section here is for any forecasts received on ship's VHF.
5. The ship notes and passage notes are for any item you wish to record about the vessel's state of health.

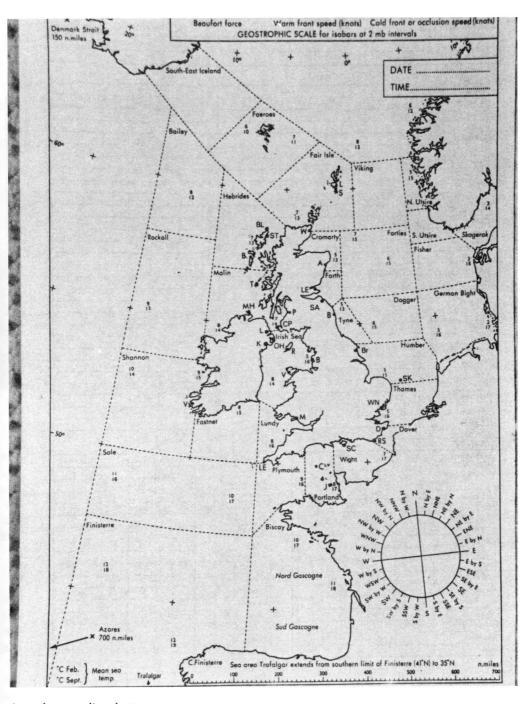

A weather recording sheet.

Side Two

This is a list of nine waypoints with spaces for serial number, lat. and long. co-ordinates, description and time of arrival. The larger squares are used to record any features which might be encountered along the leg between waypoints – for example, hazards, beacons, lighthouses, buoys and landmarks. Usually I write in the lat./long. box the co-ordinates of dangerous rocks or shoals. Then, if I am apprehensive that I might be a bit close to them, I can put this data into the GPS and get an instant picture of where I am in relation to them. It would be an unusual passage which required more than nine waypoints.

The example page from my own log (*see* the photograph on page 63) shows a sheet one which I used on passage from Lyme Regis to Cherbourg. Although the way-points are not passed through precisely, if the electronic navigators malfunction in mid-Channel or get very poor signals because of bad weather, I can use this sheet and my running log to insert an approximate position to kick-start a more rapid return to accurate function. The Decca has, for instance, played up in thunder storms several times, and even the satellite-driven GPS has been closed down without warning, when engineers have had to do work on a couple of the modules.

Completing Sheet Two

From left to right the information is:

1. Time. Always in 24-hour notation from 00.01 to 23.59. In logs, midnight does not exist because of confusion about the date on which it occurs.

2. Lat. Latitude to degrees, whole minutes and large fractions to one decimal place.
3. Long. Longitude to the same notation as lat. You only need to enter E or W if you will be crossing the Greenwich meridian.
4. The big space is for the diary. I use several lines for this. It is a mistake to be mean over space as you can never go back. I like to recall when and where the dolphins came, what big ships crossed us and at what time the fish bit well. Also in this space I put such extra information as:

(a) Course made good (CMG) – the real track over the ground.
(b) Bearing (BRG) to the next waypoint (WP).
(c) Distance (DTE) to the next WP.
(d) Course to steer (CTS) as indicated by the electronics.
(e) Cross-track error (XTE) – our distance and direction off the WP.
(f) Wilbur (the name given to my auto-pilot) – a note of the course set on the autopilot display.
(g) Cetrek – the course shown on the Cetrek fluxgate compass repeater.
(h) The engine tachometer reading (RPM).

Not all headings are used at every hour. If I change the autopilot response or yaw settings, the new ones are noted in the big space:

(a) Course as shown by the main magnetic compass (CO).
(b) Speed as given by Decca or GPS (SP).
(c) Trip distance shown on the paddle wheel log (DIST).
(d) Speed of wind in knots as shown by the anemometer, and the approximate wind direction (WIND).

(e) Barometric pressure and whether the trend is up or down (BAR).

(f) Visibility in nautical miles or fractions of nautical miles (VIS).

Exercise 7.1

Make a copy of sheet one and sheet two and fill in the appropriate spaces from the following data:

Journey Lyme Regis–Cherbourg.
Speed 6 knots.
Tide Mean is 1.5 knots E followed by W.
Wind SW4.
Dep 07.30.

There are no answers at the back for this exercise.

You Can Never Go Back

A personal foible of mine is to keep a day book. This is just a few lines written at the end of each day of a cruise, just to remind myself of what I did and where I went. It is surprising how much you forget in even a short time ashore. It is also a real treat to go back over the log and remember the times when a small bird came aboard, flew into the wheel-house, took a look at the GPS reading and flew off again – having obtained a good posfix.

I also add photographs later, and keep another log of visitors' names and addresses, to remind myself of the super people I have met whilst out sailing.

Sea Superstitions

All mariners are superstitious and there are hundreds of good luck and bad luck symbols and ideas. Below are some of the more common.

It is unlucky to start a cruise on a Friday because Christ was crucified on that day. In the nineteenth century the Royal Navy hoped to dispel this superstition by laying the keel of a new ship to be called HMS *Friday* on a Friday. She was launched on Friday and put to sea on a subsequent Friday. Neither the ship nor the crew was ever heard of again.

It is lucky to pour some wine on the deck as a libation to the Gods before setting off on a long cruise. Breaking a bottle of wine on a ship's bows at launch time derives from this superstition.

A nude woman aboard the ship makes the sea calm. This is the reason why so many ship figureheads depicted a female with breasts bared.

Swallows at sea are a good omen.

Seagulls enshroud the souls of sailors lost at sea: it is unlucky to kill one.

Count the number of fish you have caught and you won't catch any more that day.

It is unlucky to cut nails or hair at sea, because these were given as offerings to Prosperina, the Queen of Hell, and Neptune would be jealous of such offerings to another god in his kingdom.

8
ELECTRONIC
NAVIGATION

The end of the twentieth century will certainly be remembered as the 'Age of Electronics', so no navigation manual would be complete without the inclusion of electronic navigation. In spite of its importance, I have delayed writing about it until now because you cannot really 'drive' electronic navigation systems without a good grasp of chart and compass fundamentals.

There are skippers who do not agree with me on this point, and who are quite content to copy co-ordinates from lists in almanacs and then just to go where the

All the black boxes.

GPS antenna.

operator the 'Navigator' for the remainder of this chapter.

How the Enavigator Works

The scope of this book is insufficient to cope with the technical complexities of Enavigator systems. However, the basics are common to all three in general use, and even to the more esoteric methods.

The seafarer is offered the choice between Decca, Loran and the Global Positioning System (GPS). The first two depend on transmissions of radio signals from fixed stations on the land to an on-board receiver, which then sorts out transmission and reception times and plots a position from the nature of the incoming signal. GPS works from satellites and is dependent on knowing when a signal left the space station and its time of arrival at the boat. This demands extremely accurate clocks and some very high-tech computers, but the results are phenomenal.

At its simplest, all three forms use the fact that radio energy travels at approximately the speed of light, so if you know how long the radio waves have been in transit, you know how far they have travelled along a line. Most systems use a minimum of three lines to fix a position – a bit like having three rulers of different lengths pivoted at three different locations. There will be very few places where the free ends would all touch each other, but the contact would be in a position which is definable and which can be calculated.

All three Enavigator (or position-fixing) systems depend on computers for the extremely rapid processing of some large strings of numbers. The systems do a

screen arrows indicate. This is a very dangerous practice, not so much that you need a fall-back if the machine malfunctions, but more so because you need to recognize immediately when the displayed information is suspect at any point in time, or at any place along your route.

Ninety-five per cent of the errors attributed to navigational black boxes are there because the human operator fed it with poor data and had insufficient knowledge to check his or her figures.

To convey a clear differentiation between the position-fixing device and the operator – both loosely called 'navigators' – I shall name the machine the 'Enavigator' and the

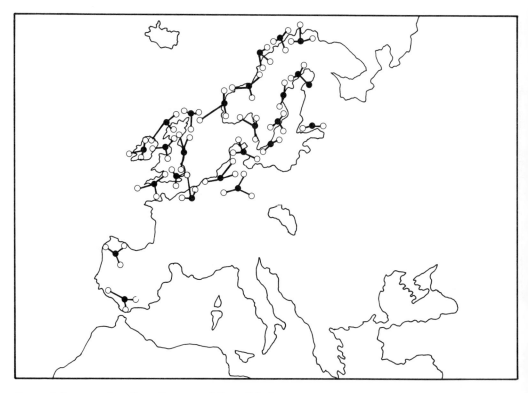

Decca chains around northern Europe and Great Britain.

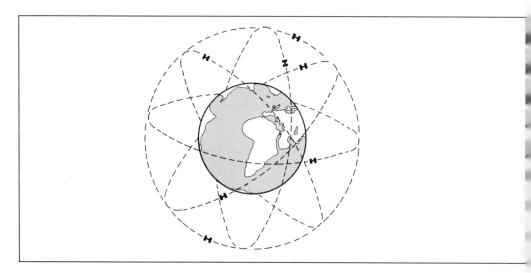

The GPS satellite Birdcage.

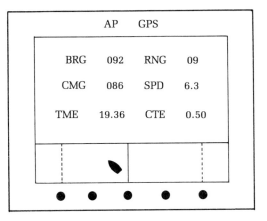

A typical Enavigator display.

number of clever things, the most important of which are listed below:

1. They fix and display the boat's position, with rapid and continuous update.

2. They can fix a series of positions at known intervals.

3. They can use this series to work out the speed and direction of travel.

4. They can give the direction and distance from the present position to any other known location.

5. They give a constant update of whether you are moving towards a known location or away from it, and at what speed and angle.

6. They can use this information to draw a plan of where the boat has been, or where it is heading and will display this on a screen.

7. They are able to show you by how much you have strayed from the straight-line course between two points.

8. They can store many reference points as latitude and longitude co-ordinates, and recall them from memory to use in any order the operator requires.

9. They can calculate your time of arrival at a known destination and will constantly revise this as your speed changes.

10. They will give audible warnings and reminders of many things, including faults and weather forecasts.

Beyond all this, the Enavigator can be interfaced with (connected to) an autopilot to take over the steering, and even to alter course on to a new heading when a certain place has been reached. As with all such powerful machines, however, you would not expect to use one without having the skills to drive it. Fortunately, you already have them, because Enavigators are fed with very basic navigational data. If it is correct they work perfectly.

Operator Error

Operator error is the most common cause of electronically-induced accidents. If the machine gives the wrong answer, it is almost always because the navigator gave it incorrect initial information – either misread the chart, or pushed the wrong button. The remedy is to check three times and input the data just once. Then, if you follow the manual/electronic double method which I have already described, you will be able to check again by comparing what the display is reading with what courses and distances you have pencilled in on the chart from your own manual efforts with dividers and plotter.

Let me admit my own fallibility here and say that one of my own worst moments of panic occurred when coming out of a Spanish harbour via a ria strewn with rocks and sandbanks. Suddenly, I realized that the visibility was closing in so that I could no longer discern any shore

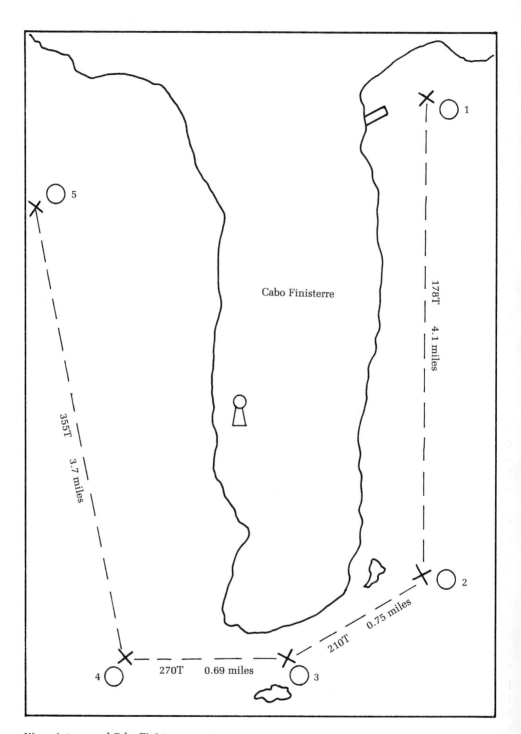

Waypoints around Cabo Finisterre.

marks, and that my reliable Decca Enavigator was saying something ridiculous about the course I should steer. The only remedy was to stop and go over all my course planning again, without haste and with no short cuts.

Inevitably, in this instance I discovered that I had typed in a couple of wrong figures. I had also left in a hurry because of a sudden change of plan, so had not followed my set routine of doing all the navigation manually and using this as a check on the Enavigator, and vice versa.

I make no apology for reiterating the message that you should double-check everything. Enavigators are super, but to rely on them totally without verifying your work is as foolish as not checking your figures when you have done a manual plot.

Waypoints

Waypoints are the Enavigator's staple diet. They are nothing more than ordinary latitude and longitude co-ordinates, which have already been used many times. The waypoint does not actually need to be a 'point along your way', it can be a buoy in the channel of your home port, a safe turning place, a hazard off to the side of your intended track, or even a spot where you once caught a lot of fish. A waypoint is therefore any sensible, recognizable latitude and longitude crossing place.

It bears repeating that experience has evolved a system whereby I draw my safe route on the chart, number each leg, and write this both on the chart and on my planning sheet. This is a task for pencil, Breton plotter and dividers. Only then do I use the parallel rule or two roller rulers to take the latitude and longitude of all my marked points. These days, I even write

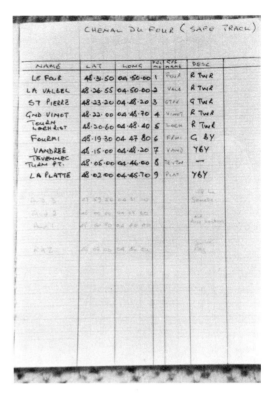

A waypoint book.

them on the chart as well as on the planning sheet. I also keep a waypoint book in case I need them again (*see* the photograph above).

The final task is to enter this data into the Enavigator memory, and to scroll through its tracks (or legs) of the course and distance between each waypoint. If these figures do not match those already written on the chart, then you have a problem. If this is the case, however, it is almost always a result of misreading or miswriting the numbers. Most commonly, I find that either the Breton plotter was misread, or the scales at the chart edges were misinterpreted, or a wrong entry key was pressed.

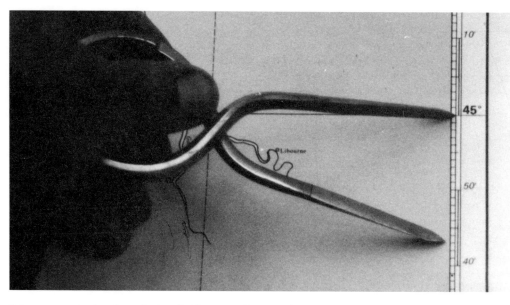

It is an easy mistake when placing dividers on a chart to subtract instead of adding.

It cannot be overemphasized that it is very dangerous to go to sea on information called out to the skipper from a navigator just reading a chart. We are all fallible, and unchecked fallibility is very dangerous indeed.

Exercise 8.1

Assume that you have drawn a safe, navigable course on the chart and have written in some of the more important courses and distances. You have also made a list of the co-ordinates of the waypoints, turning points and hazards, or other important features along the way. Some of the information on the chartlet (*see* the illustration opposite) and on the list below is incorrect. Why?

(Assume 50.40.00N 03.01.00W to be your starting point.)

1. WP00–WP01 CTS 180T/1.75NM.
2. WP02 50.36.50N 03.02.30E.
3. S hand mark is at 50.35.30N 01.75.00W.
4. WP04 50.34.50N 03.00.25W.
5. WP04–WP05 CTS 185T/2.85M.
6. WP06–50.31.20N 03.02.05W.
7. WP07 50.30.30N 03.02.30W.
8. WP08 50.30.00N 03.06.00W.

Also, answer the following questions:

9. How far are you clear of the rock at WP09?
10. What is special about the beacon mark at WP11?
11. What is the approximate course/distance to WP12?
12. What are the co-ordinates for WP12?
13. Why is WP13 well chosen?
14. What are the co-ordinates for WP14?
15. What two types of mark might be at the harbour entrance?

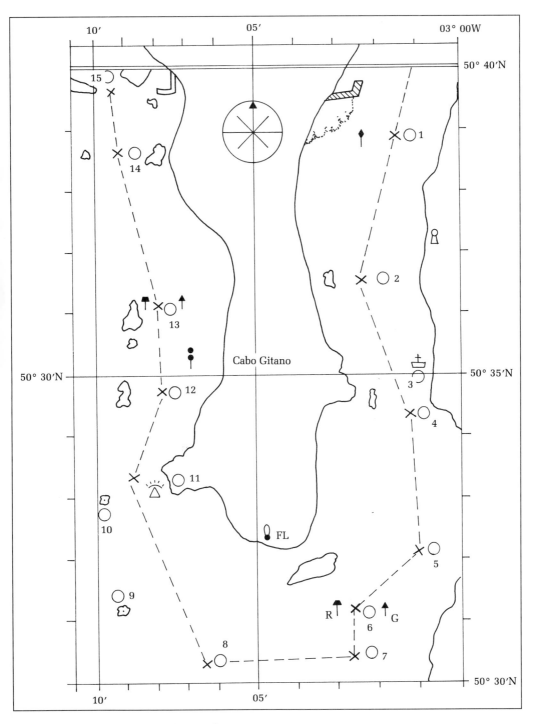

Chartlet of Cabo Gitano on a small notepad.

9
LET'S GO CRUISING

This section of our basic navigation course is both a tutorial and a test paper at the same time.

Using the information below together with the chartlets on the ensuing pages, you are invited to plan a weekend cruise from Lyme Regis around Portland Bill to Weymouth. In addition to planning, I have also set out a number of essential observations which a yacht's skipper would expect to make *en route*. This cruise is one which my own club will make this spring, so you are doing the same planning that all the boat owners will do several weeks before departure.

This long-term view must be taken for two reasons:

1.   Lyme Regis is a drying harbour, so you need to be sure that you can actually get out on Saturday and in again on Monday at reasonable times.
2.   You have to round the notorious Portland Bill which always has turbulence and overfalls, and which can have currents of up to 6 knots. Such a tide against the wind creates enormous waves and many dangers. You therefore need to time your arrival very carefully to avoid the worst of them.

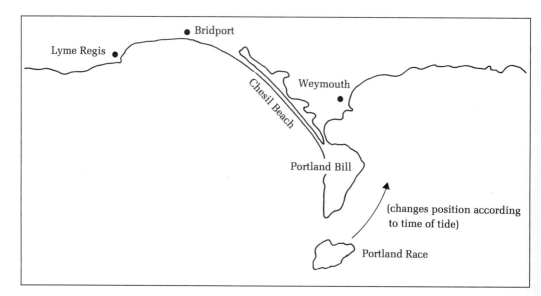

A journey from Lyme Regis to Weymouth cannot avoid the Portland race.

There are a number of other things you will need to research and calculate as part of your plan. Good sailing, and have a pleasant weekend!

Information

Sailing yacht *Valda*.
Length overall (loa) – 9m (30ft).
Beam – 2.8m (9ft 3in).
Draught – 1.5m (4ft 6in).
Rig – ketch with two headsails.
Engine – Thornycroft 55hp diesel.
Speed – 8.0 knots; 5.0 knots cruising.
Fuel – 250 litres (55 gallons); 230 litres (50 gallons) usable.
Range – 73 hours.
(**Note** The range is quoted in hours and not nautical miles. This is because sea mileage in a given time is greatly affected by favourable and adverse winds and tides.)

There are a number of things which are essential to your planning. They are encompassed by the questions which can be answered from the information in the boxes below. The major decisions are:

1. At what time can you get out of harbour?
2. What is the best time to round Portland Bill?

All other plans must be made to accommodate these important issues.

You could get all the necessary data for a real cruise from the several nautical annuals, of which the *Macmillan and Silk Cut Almanac* or *Reed's Nautical Almanac* are the best known. For this theoretical purpose, however, I have given a much more simple set of navigation facts than

---

LYME REGIS HARBOUR

Relevant charts
Admiralty 3315 Portland Bill to Berry Head, Imray C05.

Standard port for tidal reference – Devonport.
Mean time difference on Devonport – HW + 00.50, LW 00.00.
Mean height difference on Devonport – HW – 1.3m, LW – 0.3m.

Berthing
Anchorage is permitted on buoys outside harbour. Alongside berths inside harbour dry out at all low waters. Space is limited by fishing trawlers. Shelter is good from all directions except E–NE.

Pilotage
Safe waypoint is 50.43.10N 02.55.70W. Breakwater is marked by red basket on pole. Leading lights Occ 8s 296. Beware lobster pots around harbour entrance and approaches.

Communications
Harbourmaster on VHF channel 16/14. Tel. (0297) 442137.

Facilities
Fresh water on quay. Marine engineer available. Yacht club open Wednesday and Saturday evenings in season. Some chandlery. Launderette in town. There are no showers and no fuel close to hand.

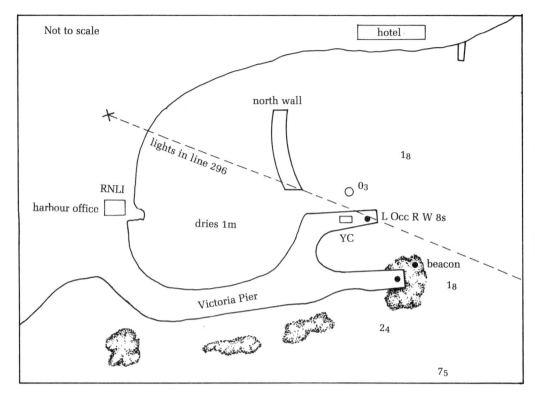

Plan of Lyme Regis harbour.

these tomes contain, and have not made the information relate to any particular day or to any real day's tides.

Exercise 9.1

Note Round off all times to nearest convenient figures.

1. What is the time of HW Devonport?
2. Is this UTC, GMT or local time?
3. What is the tidal range at Devonport?
4. Is HW Lyme Regis Devonport plus or minus?
5. How do you write this in tide table notation?
6. What is the time of HW Lyme Regis?

TIDAL INFORMATION

Devonport at tide station 50.22.00N 04.11.00W.

Saturday 6 May
05.25 – 5.2m   11.30 – 0.8m
17.45 – 5.3m   23.45 – 0.8m

Notes:
Maximum range at Devonport is 0.8–5.3m.
Minimum range at Devonport is 1.8–4.4m.
Range at Lyme Regis on 6 May is 0.6–4.1.

7. How much water will be at the anchorage at 12.30?

8. What is the latest time *Valda* can leave harbour?

9. How would you get a pre-cruise radio check?

10. What are the directions to steer and what are the harbour light characteristics if you return after dark on Monday?

Rounding Portland Bill

The most important part of the journey is the rounding of Portland Bill. We do not wish to add 12nm to our journey by passing outside the race, so hope to go around at about 200m out, from where we shall be able to see the nests of the Portland parrots (the local name for seagulls). The turbulent part of the race moves during the course of a tidal cycle. We need to avoid this and also to avoid fast-running counter-tides.

There is plenty of information on Portland Bill to be found in the almanacs and from more local sources. Sailing clubs have their own chartlets derived from experience, and the local fishermen also have their own knowledge which they are always willing to share with anyone who asks for help.

Exercise 9.2

1. What is the rhumb-line course from Lyme Regis to Portland Bill?

2. What is the rhumb-line distance from Lyme Regis to Portland Bill?

3. How would you get these two pieces of information?

4. Will you sail the rhumb-line or sail a course inside the bay?

5. What is your reason for this?

PORTLAND BILL

Portland Bill is the southern tip of the Isle of Portland, which is joined to the mainland by a shingle causeway. There is deep water right in close to the headland itself, but because it juts out into the tide it causes a huge current acceleration. Where the east-going flood tide meets the west-going ebb tide, overfalls and whirlpools appear. The Portland race varies in position according to the tide and can reach speeds of 7.5 knots.

There is an inshore passage to about 350m (383yd) of the cliffs, or the yacht must pass about 5 nautical miles to seaward.

The best times to round Portland Bill are:

Going east – HW Devonport minus 02.00 approximately.

Going west – HW Devonport plus 04.00 approximately.

This will give smooth water and a favourable tide once the headland has been rounded.

Distances
Lyme Regis to Portland Bill – 22nm.
Portland Bill to Weymouth – 8nm.

6. What is the approximate running time to Portland Bill at 5 knots?

7. At what time will you plan to depart Lyme Regis?

8. With 5 knots of boat speed, what speed will you make on the east side of Portland Bill?

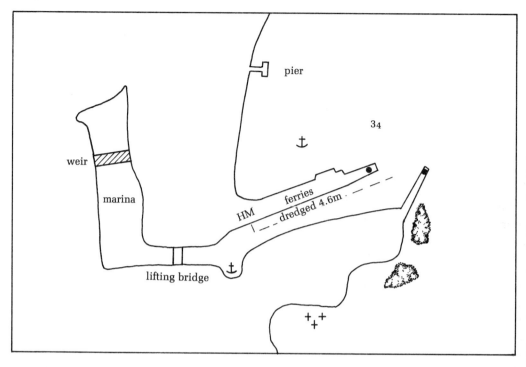

Plan of Weymouth harbour.

9. What is your ETA at Weymouth?
10. Who will you inform of this and by what means?
11. What are the characteristics of Portland Bill Lighthouse?
12. How much water will be at the entrance to Weymouth?

13. What hazards would you expect near Portland Bill?
14. What hazards occur between Portland Bill and Weymouth?
15. What pilotage precautions would you take at Weymouth harbour entrance?

10

THE RULES OF
THE ROAD

The rules for avoiding collision at sea are a paradox of complex simplicity. They are complex because the traffic is not constrained by kerbs and hedges, but can go two-dimensionally wherever it pleases (except when it is in agreed shipping lanes, or in an area known as a traffic separation scheme). They are also simple because once you appreciate their logic, the few anti-collision regulations deemed necessary are quite clear cut.

The rules are now universal and are agreed by the International Maritime Organisation (IMO). They are too long to be here quoted in their entirety, but begin with a deal of common sense, which can be enforced by law and punished with heavy fines. All vessels are required to keep a good look out at all times and not to take any action, or to insist on their theoretical rights, if this puts another vessel into danger – for example, causing it to run into shallow water, or causing it to collide with a third party. They also stress the need for speed commensurate with conditions of visibility, population and the closeness of boats being used for work.

Apart from this general rule, the specific rules state that:

1. When two sailing boats are on

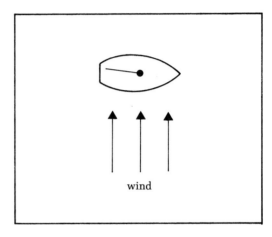

This yacht is on a starboard tack.

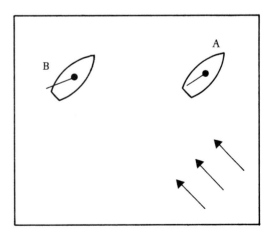

Boat A is to windward of boat B.

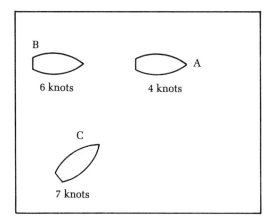

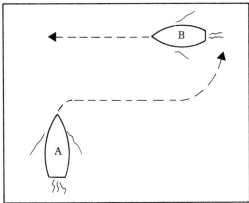

Both boat B and boat C are overtaking boat A and must take avoiding action. Boat A must maintain its course and speed.

Two vessels crossing. Boat A must alter its course to pass port to port astern of boat B, which must stand on.

collision course, the one with the wind on its port side keeps clear. If they both have the wind on the same side, the up-wind boat keeps clear.

2.   A vessel overtaking another must give it plenty of sea room and is required to give way. Overtaking means getting closer from an angle of more than 22½° aft of her beam, or within the sector of her stern light at night. The overtaken vessel must hold its course and speed without alteration.

3.   When two power-driven vessels approach head on, both are required to alter course to starboard and to allow the other to pass down the port side. They are also advised to make the appropriate sound signal.

4.   When two powered vessels are crossing each other, the vessel with the other on its starboard side should keep clear and avoid passing ahead of the other. The vessel not required to give way has a duty to 'stand on' – in other words, it must not confuse the situation by taking evasive action.

These two recommendations are the foundation of the sea's rules. It comes down to a question of what you are seeing and what part of your own hull, or colour of light, you are showing to the other boat.

5.   Additionally, power boats give way to sailing vessels, and all craft keep clear of vessels engaged in fishing, or those either not under command or restricted in manoeuvrability by size or draught.

Two power vessels on a collision course. Each must alter to starboard.

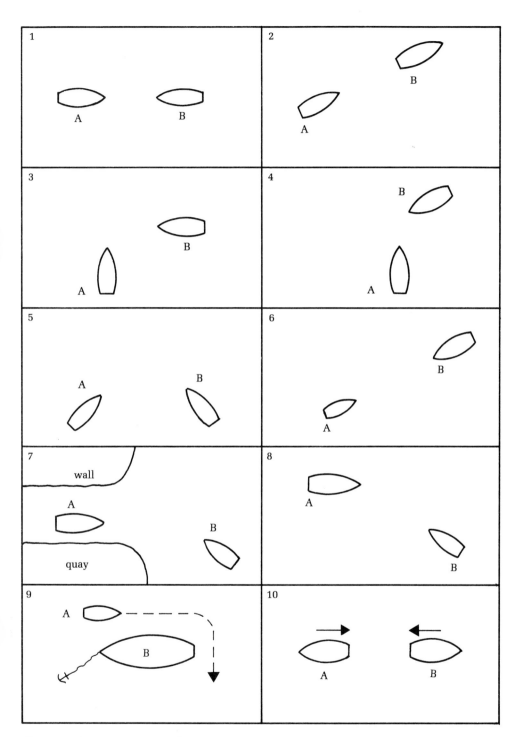

Illustration for Exercises 10.1 and 10.2.

In general, the leisure boater will most often be required to make judgements about the so-called port to port, or red to red rules. It is these which will provide the answers to the question situations below.

Exercise 10.1

Use the illustration on page 83 for this exercise. All diagrams are deemed to be north up. In answering, you may give your course of action as 'alter course east', 'turn to starboard' or 'slow down'.

Imagine that you are the skipper of vessel A. What is your proper course of action in each of the ten common situations given in the illustration?

Exercise 10.2

Use the same illustration that you used for Exercise 10.1, and repeat the series, but imagine this time that you are the master of craft B. What is the course of action in each of the ten situations?

Sound Signals

Because ships can appear to be turning slowly – and even not to be turning at all when viewed from some angles – there is a code of sound signals that tells everybody around what it is about to do. This is a very simple, logical, communications method of blasts on the klaxon, hooter or siren, beginning with one short transmission for the most usual thing a helmsman does – alter course to starboard.

The sound signal code consists of a dot (.) or a short blast of about one second on a klaxon or a foghorn, and a dash (–), or a long blast of at least four seconds by the same means. Signals for vessels in sight of each other (generally manoeuvring in harbour) are as follows:

.	I am altering course to starboard.
. .	I am altering course to port.
. . .	My engines are going astern (possibly to stop the boat).
– – .	I intend to overtake on your starboard side.
– – . .	I intend to overtake on your port side.
– . – .	I agree to your overtaking intentions.
. . . . .	(a) I fail to understand your intentions. (b) I do not think that you are taking sufficient avoiding action.
———	Warning given by large vessel approaching a channel bend.

Poor visibility and fog signals are separate from those given above.

Exercise 10.3

Refer to the illustration opposite for this exercise. (The dotted line is the intended action and all diagrams are north up.) Imagine that you are the skipper of vessel A. What sound signal would you make in each of the situations given in the illustration?

Exercise 10.4

Refer to the illustration used for Exercise 10.3 for this exercise. (The dotted line is the intended action and all diagrams are north up.) Imagine that you are the skipper of vessel B. What sound signal would you make in each of the situations given in the illustration?

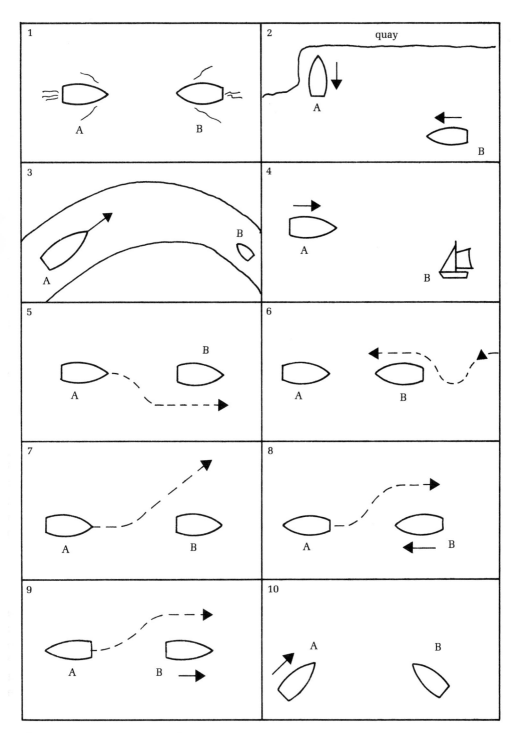

Illustration for Exercises 10.3 and 10.4.

11
LET'S HAVE AN
ADVENTURE

As soon as you have completed a few successful coastal passages, a trip to another country begins to beckon. For most of us who live in the United Kingdom, the logical first destination is France. The English Channel sits there like a challenge, which most boat owners hope to face. In this chapter we will not sail to the usual destinations in France. Instead, we shall make the longer passage

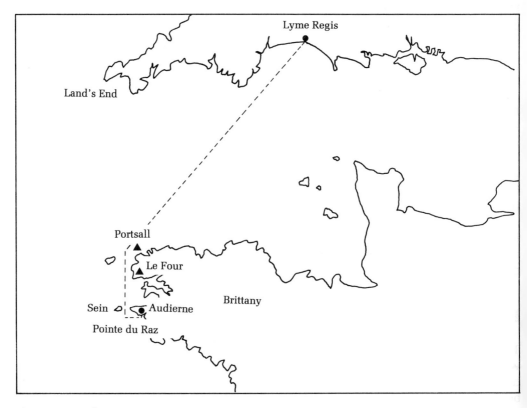

The route to Audierne.

Lyme Regis harbour.

from Lyme Regis around Finistère, France's most western mainland tip, down past Ushant and around the corner of Brittany to the delightful little town of Audierne, with its snug harbour, fresh bread on the quay and a daily market just fifty metres from the boat's berth.

Planning such a major boat expedition is divided into a number of phases, beginning at least six months before the off.

Phase One

This consists of a feasibility study as to whether the crew and boat can make the trip in the time allowed. It looks at what books, almanacs, pilotage publications, charts and other information is available.

During these early days, I also collect such material as relevant back issues of magazines discussing the area, look at the Cruising Association Library list and write to tourist offices for their brochures.

Phase Two

Phase two is a rough guide, done about two months before D-day. Now is the time to pencil in the route lightly on the passage chart, to have a first look at tides for getting off the berth and for traversing the 'significant' points.

All passages have at least one significant point (remember Portland Bill?). In this case we have five:

1. Getting out of a tidal harbour.

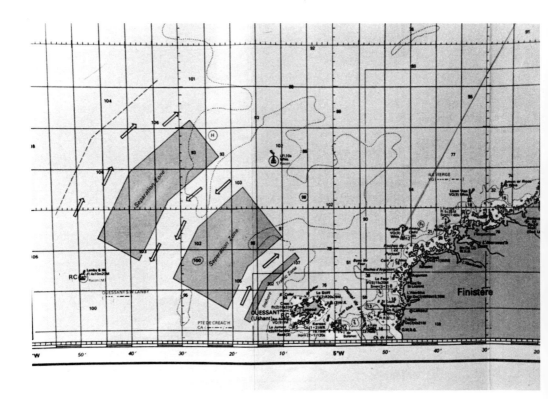

The Ushant Traffic Separation Scheme.

2. Crossing the shipping lanes and any obligatory traffic separation schemes.

3. The need to be at Le Four Lighthouse at exactly HW Brest.

4. The dangers of hitting Le Raz de Sein at the wrong time.

5. Whether we shall be able to get up the river at Audierne, for a calm pontoon berth after such a long passage.

For the Lyme Regis to Audierne passage, our planning needs to be worked back from Le Four. The tide runs very hard in this channel, so we need to be going with it. If we get the timing wrong at this point, we shall be forced to divert into one of the refuge harbours adjacent to the route.

Phase Three

Phase three is very much the nuts and bolts of the planning process. It happens a few days before setting sail. It encompasses waypoints, courses, detailed notes on tides, estimated running times and a final, very comprehensive, imaginary passage along the whole route to check all the data and to make notes of hazards, lights, buoys and emergency, bad weather shelter ports.

Assuming phases one and two have been completed, the information below should enable you to plan the passage in detail by working through the exercises.

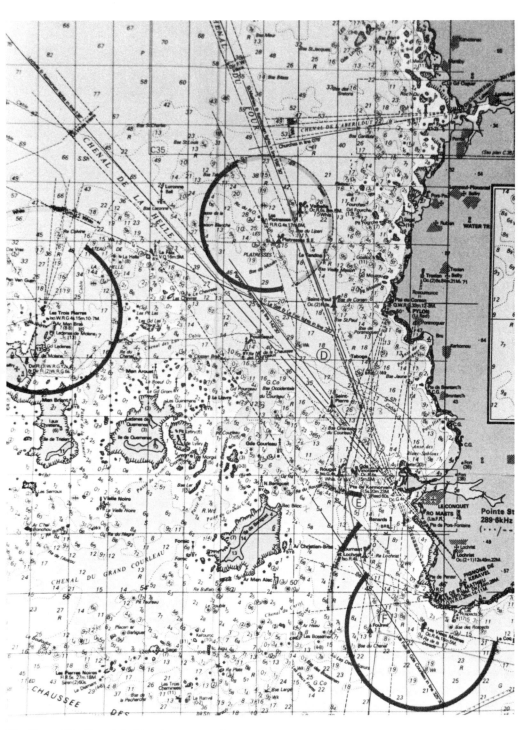

The Chart of Le Chenal du Four is very complex.

Passage planning is always a matter of making a cocktail of information from ingredients gathered from a number of sources. When he or she is in 'planning mode', the navigator's desk is covered with charts and reference books. At best, the navigator operates in 'overkill' – his or her passage notes contain the maximum amount of information, so that it is ready to hand. As a navigator, you do not want to be diving around several books for data which is needed in a hurry, when it is dark, or when the boat is tossing about in a rough sea. To answer the questions in the following exercises you too will need to 'dive' around the information boxes.

There are plenty of charts and books to help.

BOAT SPECIFICATIONS

Sailing yacht *Valda*.
Length overall (loa) – 9m (30ft).
Beam – 2.8m (9ft 3in).
Draught – 1.5m (4ft 6in).
Rig – ketch with two headsails.
Engine – Thornycroft 55hp diesel.
Speed – 8.0 knots; 5.0 knots cruising.
Fuel – 250 litres (55 gallons), 230 litres (50 gallons) usable.
Range – 73 hours.

Expected date of departure – Sunday 19 May.

AVAILABLE CHARTS

Imray C10 Western English Channel (passage chart).
Imray C34 Cap d'Erquy to Ile de Batz.
Imray C35 Baie de Morlaix to l'Aberildut.
Imray C36 Ile d'Ouessant to Raz de Sein.
Imray C37 Raz de Sein to Benodet.

Also available are several nautical almanacs, Lyme Regis tide tables (Nigel J. Clarke Publications) and the south Brittany pilot.

TIDAL INFORMATION

Tides at Lyme Regis on 19 May

05.21 – 1.7m.   17.55 – 1.9m.
11.53 – 4.4m.   range – 2.6m.

Maximum HW in May – 4.9m.
Minimum LW in May – 0.8m.

Tides at Brest
Time Zone – 0100 (subtract 1 hour for GMT/UTC).

Monday 20 May	Tuesday 21 May
06.15 – 2.4m	00.59 – 6.4m
12.24 – 6.1m	07.24 – 2.2m
18.50 – 2.4m	13.32 – 6.4m
	19.55 – 2.1m

Maximum range for May is HW 7.6m, LW 1.1m.
Minimum range for May is HW 5.6m, LW 3.1m.

High Water Dover

Sunday: 19.05	Monday: 20.05
00.45 – 4.2m	06.08 – 4.1m
17.20 – 4.0m	18.38 – 4.0m
07.20 – 4.4m	19.42 – 4.4m

Maximum range for Dover in May is HW 6.5m, LW 0.9m.
Minimum range for Dover in May is HW 5.1m, LW 2.1m.

CHENAL DU FOUR

The Chenal du Four is a twisting channel passing between Ushant and the French mainland. It is usable by large ships and is well marked by buoys, beacons and lights. It is also well monitored by the radar stations on either side.

The problem with Le Four is that the ground is uneven, and this combines with a geographic squeeze to produce very fast running tides, with dangerous overfalls if the wind and tide are against each other. A yacht drawing less than 1.8m (6ft) could make the passage down from Le Four Lighthouse in a straight line, but prudent skippers use the channel and its marks as extra navigational fixes, and to be assured of the deepest water.

Aim to arrive opposite Le Four Lighthouse at just before HW Brest. At this time, you will have slack water and should thereafter be able to use the ebb to carry you down to the notorious Raz de Sein on one tide. You should then be able to negotiate the Raz at slack water.

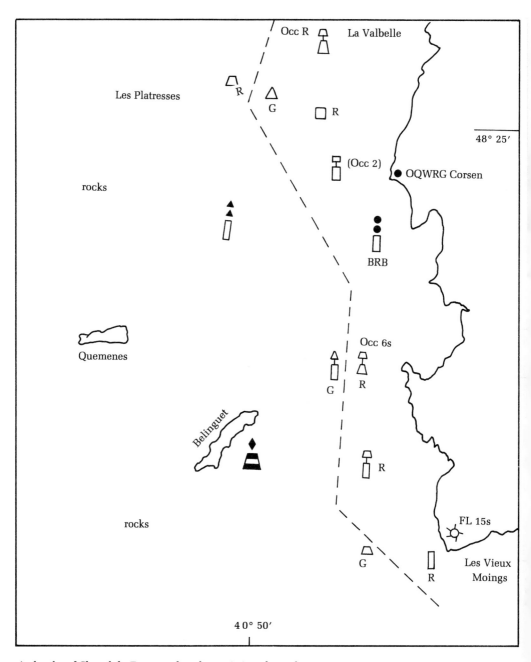

A chartlet of Chanel du Four – a deep but twisting channel.

RAZ DE SEIN

The Raz de Sein is a narrow passage between La Pointe du Raz and the island of the same name. Its evil reputation as one of the most dangerous corners in Europe is well deserved, but it does not present problems to a well-found boat being navigated 'on the clock'. In calm conditions, a power boat can get through the Raz at any stage of the tide. Less powerful vessels should aim to pass at the slack water on either side of HW or LW. For practical pilotage purposes, this can be taken to occur at the same time as HW and LW for Brest.

USEFUL WAYPOINTS EN ROUTE

Rhumb line at 40nm – 50.09N 03.32W.
Rhumb line at 80nm – 49.49N 03.58W.
Rhumb line at 120nm – 48.59N 04.29W.
Portsall Buoy – 48.38.50N 04.46.50W.

AUDIERNE

Audierne is a charming little port situated in the tidal estuary of the River Goyen. There is a yacht harbour with pontoons, chandlery and all other amenities, including two large supermarkets. There is a daily vegetable and meat market in Les Halles. Petrol and diesel fuel are transported from a garage in the town.

Audierne can only be reached at HW plus or minus two hours. If you miss the tide in the river, there are ample visitors' buoys at Saint Evette, just outside the harbour entrance. Diesel fuel is also available here.

The Audierne contact is via La Mairie. It has no radio communications.

Tides times are Brest minus 00.30. Tidal heights are Brest MHWS – 2.3, MLWS – 0.5, MHWN – 1.9, MLWN – 1.4. (MHWS is mean high water spring, MLWS is mean low water spring, MHWN is mean high water neap, and MLWN is mean low water neap.)

DISTANCE

Lyme Regis to Portsall – 145nm.
Portsall to Le Four – 06nm.
Le Four to Raz de Sein – 30nm.
Raz de Sein to Audierne – 08nm.

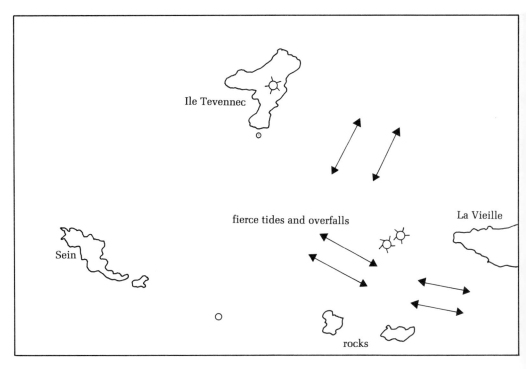

Ile Tevennec

fierce tides and overfalls

La Vieille

Sein

rocks

Chartlet of the Raz de Sein – it may look easy, but the tide can reach speeds of up to 10 knots.

CHENAL DU FOUR SAFE PASSAGE

Le Four	– 48.31.50N 04.50.00W (red tower).
La Valbelle	– 48.26.55N 04.50.00W (red tower).
Sainte Pierre	– 48.23.20N 04.28.20W (green tower).
Grande Vinotière	– 48.22.00N 04.48.70W (red tower).
Tourn Lochcrist	– 48.20.00N 04.48.40W (red tower).
Fourmi	– 48.19.30N 04.47.80W (green buoy).
Vandrée	– 48.15.00N 04.48.20W (YBY).
La Plate	– 48.02.00N 04.45.70W (YBY).

Table 6.

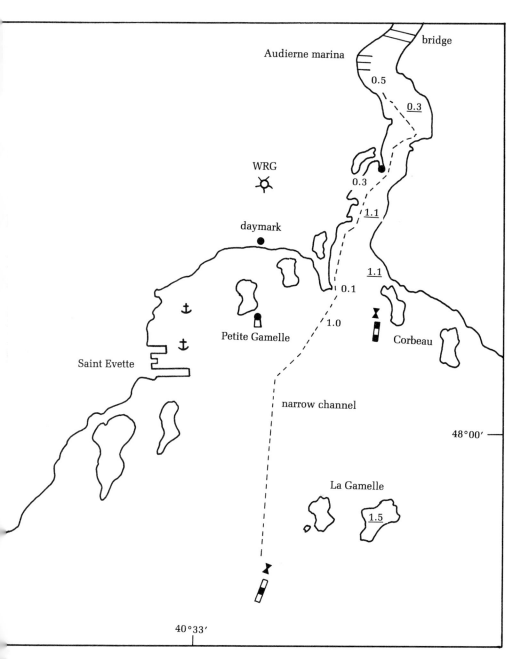

hartlet of Audierne – a berth here depends on the tide.

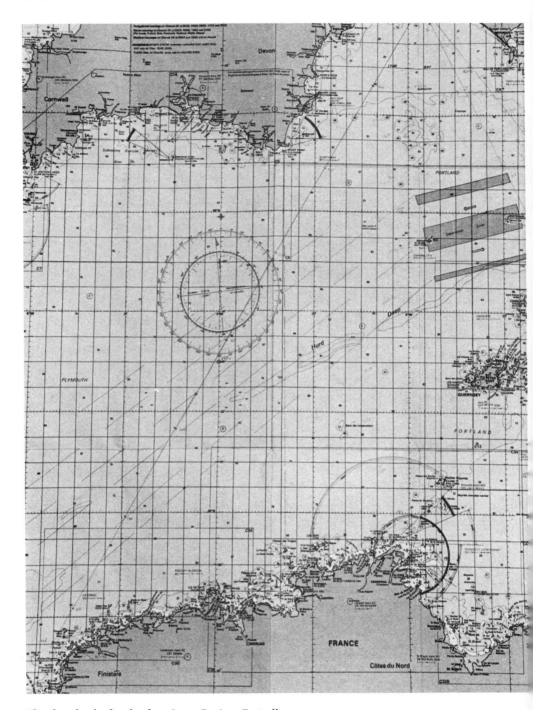

The chart for the first leg from Lyme Regis to Portsall.

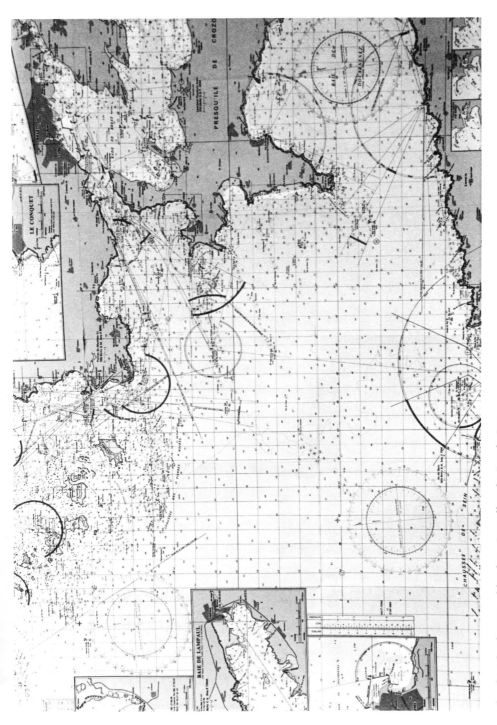

The chart for the second leg from Portsall to the Raz de Sein.

The chart for the third leg from the Raz de Sein to Audierne.

Exercise 11.1 – The Departure

1. What is *Valda*'s draught in metres?
2. What will be her running time to Portsall?
3. What is the running time to Le Four?
4. What is the earliest afternoon time you can leave harbour?
5. What is the latest time you can leave harbour?
6. How much 'safety time' will you allow?
7. To whom and by what means will you give details of your passage?
8. What details will you give?
9. Will you inform anyone else that you are going?
10. When would you expect it to get dark on Sunday 10 May?

Exercise 11.2 – Across the Channel

1. What is the rhumb-line course to Portsall?
2. What will you set on the compass?
3. When you see the first very big ships, on which side of the boat should they appear?
4. At about what time do you expect to see them?
5. If one comes close, what action will you take?
6. What principal usable lighthouses will be visible *en route*?
7. What navigation mark is at Portsall?
8. What are the colour, topmark and light characteristics of this mark?
9. What is your optimum ETA at Portsall?
10. What is the local time of HW Brest?

Exercise 11.3 – Le Chenal du Four

Write up your passage notes for Le Chenal du Four. List principal marks, course between them, distance and running time. (Assume a boat speed of 5 knots and a tide of 2 knots 180°T.) Follow the layout below:

Le Four	Large red tower	0.5nm port
CSE 190T	Distance 05nm	Time 43 minutes
La Valbelle	Red tower	100m Stbd

Continue via La Valbelle, Les Platresses, Saint Paul, Saint Pierre, Grande Vinotière, Fourmi, Vandrée and La Plate (Raz de Sein).

Exercise 11.4 – Le Raz de Sein to Audierne

1. How will you recognize La Plate?
2. If you are late/early at the Raz, what will you do?
3. What is An Hinkinou?
4. What are the approximate course and distance from Raz to Audierne?
5. What is your ETA at Audierne?
6. Will the tide be with you or against on this leg?
7. At what time can you get up the river?
8. There are three marks with the name Gamelle. What do they tell you?
9. Where would you expect the biggest problem in going up the river?
10. What type of berth is at Audierne?

Exercise 11.5 – General Seamanship

1. What HM Customs procedure is required before departure?
2. What ship's papers should you carry?
3. What personal documents are required?
4. What weather information will you get *en route*?
5. How can you check on free berths at Audierne?
6. Who will you contact on arrival?
7. What officials would you expect to come aboard?
8. Assume that you sail for half the time, motor for half, and use 2.3 litres per hour (0.5 gph). How much fuel will you use?
9. Will you fly the yellow customs flag on arrival?
10. What other flags, if any, are obligatory?

The Traditional Sea Gods

Neptune is the king of the Oceans, usually pictured as a stately, bearded old man carrying a trident and sitting astride a dolphin or an animal called the hippocampus, having the tail of a fish and the head of a horse. Alternatively he is shown with a dolphin in one hand and a trident in the other, with his feet resting on part of a ship. Neptune (Poseidon to the Greeks) was believed to use his trident to make or calm storms, to shatter rocks and to shake the shores. He lived in a golden palace on the seabed and when his horses with golden manes drew his chariots over the sea the water became as smooth as glass. The ancients believed that Neptune invented the horse and his effigy is still sometimes used as a patron of horse races.

Calypso a beautiful sea nymph, the daughter of Atlas, living in a grotto of vines and flowers. She tried to make Ulysses live with her for ever and to become immortal, but Zeus commanded her to let him go.

Triton is usually represented as a fish or a dolphin from the waist down and blowing on a shell, which action was said to cause the roaring of the ocean. Triton was Neptune's trumpeter.

12
FINAL DESTINATION

If you have worked steadily through the book, you should now be competent and comfortable in the basics of each of the separate, normal navigational skills. Those crafts and sciences which you have learned are the ones which I use all day and every day of my cruising life. These fundamentals cannot be avoided, but you have actually done more than simply understand these basics. In fact, the two cruises which you have planned are two which I shall personally undertake this year.

It gets lonely aboard a small boat on such a vast ocean, but there is always something to do. The actual task of navigating, of constantly checking position by a variety of means, occupies about 50 per cent of this work. Writing up the log every hour and taking regular weather forecasts also eat into time when you may have hoped to read novels, do crosswords and listen to music. The navigator does not have time to become bored.

About here, you may well point out that I have not mentioned astro-navigation – the method of fixing position with a sextant, the sun and the stars. There are a number of reasons for the omission, not least that this is a book for beginners. Let me also confess that I have not needed to take my sextant out of its box for operational reasons for several years now. The one time I felt that I might need it, I did not see the sun and stars for several days. Instead, I relied on the basic skills of

dead reckoning and then checked my position from a radio direction-finder when I got closer to land. From there in it was eyeball navigation – the basics again.

Another reason for not dabbling in astro-navigation here is because, even with computer programs to do all the number crunching, it is still quite complex. The pains of introducing students to astro-navigation too early have probably been more responsible for them giving up on navigation classes than any other factor. This trauma has often been aggravated by tutors guarding and glamorizing the mystique behind it and giving astro-navigation the status of one of the 'black arts'.

This is to be regretted, because above all navigation should be fun for the leisure boat user. If your enthusiasm is for charts and rulers, whether you like calculators and Enavigator gadgets, or if you love a combination of all four it does not matter. There are still few better feelings or reasons for satisfaction afloat than making a difficult passage well, and always knowing exactly where you are and precisely where you are going. 'It all checks out', is one of the most welcome phrases aboard my own motor-sailer.

I hope that you have enjoyed working this book as much as I have enjoyed researching and compiling it. Stay cool and stay well, and may your landmarks always be where you expect them.

13
REVISION CLASS

The ground rules of navigation should now be familiar enough for you to be a competent boat pilot. Yet navigation – and writing about the black arts of marine pilotage – is no different from most other areas of human endeavour. The pattern is usually a wheel, so anything on its circumference always returns to its starting point. The same applies to my own boat and the way I get it from place to place. It is very comprehensively equipped with electronic navigation aids and sprouts more aerials than the average warship, but oddly enough, the more I use these miracles of modern technology, the more often I have to inject skills derived from very basic, traditional precepts, and use the short cuts which follow to manipulate them more easily. Whatever the advantages of modern technology, you will still need the use of your eyes and your brain. Even though I have installed three position-fixing and course-indicating systems, plus a radio direction finder, digital sounder, video sounder, distance log, speed log, digital compass repeater, radar, computer, calculator and chart plotter, I cannot use them well without a high input of knowledge and a dose of mental arithmetic.

As inaccurate number crunching can seriously damage your physical and mental health, and as any serious mistakes can be fatal, I have developed an armoury of checks and balances, plus short cuts

All the traditional instruments are still needed.

and easy routes to keep my sanity and t enable me to think on my feet whilst tryin, to keep my balance on a bouncing boa Sometimes this brainwork needs to b done very quickly. Amongst the best o these tricks is the habit of making approx imations constantly – in other words reducing complex numbers to mentall manageable figures and using other factors to check against total stupidities. However, in order to benefit from this, you must get into the habit of always making and stating the mental liaisons.

Compass Simplification

Handling compass three-figure notation is a good example of where you can benefit from simple checks. I, for instance, still do not have an immediate clear mental picture of where a heading of 225 will take me. But if I always say to myself 'Course 225 is south-west', I avoid any terrible errors. Such mistakes can happen and have happened to most of us who cruise seriously. A wrong figure could tell you to steer 185 instead of 285 and the result could be a wrecked boat – unless you say something constantly like, 'Course 185 is nearly south, but I should be heading nearly north-west, so something is wrong'.

On my boat, courses as such 271 or 267 only exist on the electronic screens. In practical pilotage terms and in conversation, they both become 'West! Two seven zero.' This gives a much simpler mental picture to visualize and to retain in your mind.

Approximate Conversions

There are occasions when a navigator needs to make a conversion from one unit to another – changing between inches and centimetres, or from metres and kilometres to nautical miles are the most usual. A little later on I shall talk about memory cards and calculators, but most navigators carry some reference conversions in their head. Typical of mine are that 200m equals 1 nautical mile, that 8km equals 5 miles and that 50 miles equals 80km.

Before you carry out any mental arithmetic or jotter pad conversion, you should always ask yourself whether the result should be a larger figure or a smaller. In a conversion there will always be fewer miles than kilometres and always more metres than fathoms. This is a small tip, but can be a real boon when your brain is very tired.

Time Approximation

In the real world, such time precision as 11.29 is something of a nonsense, as is 11.58. To the navigator both of these can be noted to the nearest half-hour – in other words 11.30 and 12.00. Likewise, you can complicate both tidal and passage information by sticking to some such time as 23.57 if you are adding hours, or 00.12 if you are subtracting. Both involve changing day and date as well as time. In the case of the former, it would be much simpler to add twenty-four hours and thirty-five minutes from midnight and then to fine tune the result by three extra minutes if you really must.

This type of problem is usually associated with tidal calculations such as needing to know the time of half-tide, or with an estimated time of arrival (ETA) displayed by GPS. You can round up both to the nearest quarter of an hour for two reasons: nobody can correctly forecast the tide to anything like a minute, or even ten centimetres; and the ETA will alter as the boat's speed is affected by wind and tide. In the very nature of things we are only making rough estimates, so approximate arithmetic will suffice.

Tide tables are marvellously detailed, but you can use them in approximate form too.

Exercise 13.1

Add or subtract the indicated hours and minutes to the times below. By using approximations you should be able to complete the test in less than sixty seconds.

1. 17.27 + 2h 59m
2. 23.55 + 4h 57m
3. 12.32 + 3h 32m
4. 13.14 + 2h 13m
5. 15.17 – 2h 13m
6. 23.58 – 1h 29m
7. 12.03 – 3h 01m
8. 12.03 – 2h 58m
9. 16.44 + 0h 32m
10. 11.02 – 6h 02m

If you really wish to be punctilious, you could adjust the minutes afterwards as simple, single-figure arithmetic. When doing the above with a pocket calculator, enter the fractions of an hour in decimal notation – in other words, 17.15 = 17.25, 17.30 = 17.50, 17.45 = 17.75.

Tidal Approximations

The suggestions applying to time approximation should also be used to make tidal mental arithmetic easier, especially as the height and time of the tide are much influenced by atmospheric pressure and by weather effects – for example, a gale the day before, or even a strong blow in the next sea area. Tides are also subject to local peculiarities. In my home port, for instance, the transition from ebb to recommencement of the flood is so immediate that you can almost see it happening but, on some tides, there can be a high water stand of almost an hour.

These are conditions on the shore, but once you get about two miles out to sea, there is always a period of slack water straddling the times two hours before local high water and four hours after the predicted time for the 'top of the tide' on shore. This information is essential to fishermen and divers, but it still remains that tidal times and levels are an instance where 'near enough is good enough'. In spite of computerized predictions and tidal calculations, if you can estimate a tide to within 10cm of its true level, you are lucky – even 25cm is not too bad.

When you note a tide's height and range from an almanac, it is quite safe to round up LW 1.99m to the whole number of 2m, or to round back HW 7.06m to the whole number of 7m. The range for that tide can then be calculated and used as 5m.

Exercise 13.2

Give the approximate range for the first ten days of an imaginary month as shown below. Allow yourself sixty seconds.

1.	01.46 – 09.44.	6.	01.01 – 07.03.
2.	00.97 – 10.98.	7.	02.06 – 04.02.
3.	02.24 – 07.31	8.	01.99 – 10.74.
4.	01.03 – 06.49.	9.	02.25 – 10.76.
5.	01.03 – 06.52.	10.	02.55 – 10.55.

Note on Rule of Twelfths

Even though I was recently – and rather pompously – told by one non-boat owning instructor of a nationally organized course that he no longer teaches the 'Rule of Twelfths' because it has been outmoded by almanac tidal graphs and calculators which are more precise, I still continue to practise it. There are many times when bad weather makes a skipper divert to a strange port and at such times he does not want to have to go below to look at a tidal curve graph – even if he can get the almanac to stay on the table. There are also times when a pocket calculator is not to hand, or when you do not want to risk using it in a spray-drenched cockpit. At such times it is very useful to work in approximations and to use the Rule of Twelfths as described in Chapter 5.

Chartwork Approximation

For 'at a glance' navigation as the boat is underway, it is very useful to have an approximate idea of the chart's scale in terms of miles to the inch or centimetre. It is often interesting, useful or even essential to know roughly how far off a buoy, hazard or headland your rhumb-line course will take you, but not always convenient or necessary to get out the dividers. At such times, you can 'guesstimate' distance by stepping the measurement across to the latitude scale with your fingers or, better still, by knowing facts such as that 1in equals 2 miles or whatever.

The scale of the chart in use is always noted amongst the header information. In my own case, I actually write on the edge of the chart that, say, at 1:50,000 1in equals roughly 0.7m and at 1:75,000 1in is

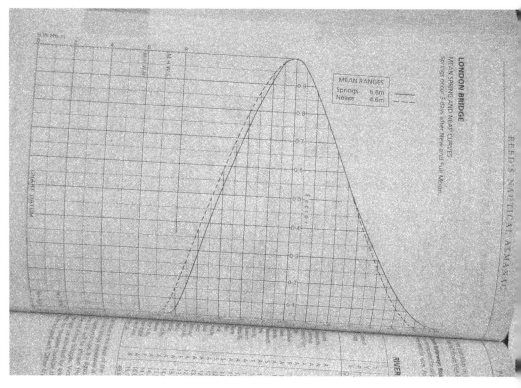

Tidal curve – accurate but needs a steady boat.

equivalent to a touch over 1 mile. I can then use my thumb as an approximate inch, or use the roller rule. Other skippers keep a memo card which gives the appropriate single unit distance for all the charts and chartlets in their library.

You should also soon get into the habit of using the grid lines printed on the chart as approximate posfix aids. If your Decca/GPS reads 50.39.15N, you might be just 1in below the 50.40.00N line on a 1:75,000 scale chart.

Chartwork should be such fun that skippers who are alert will feed themselves constantly with this sort of estimated information about position and about distance to be covered at present speed.

Chart Corrections

Any alterations to charts, buoys and so on are published in weekly 'Notices to Mariners' issued by the Hydrographer to the Navy and printed in digest form by some yachting journals. In common with many other boat owners, I have neither the time nor the patience to put in all these alterations every month, so usually ink in only the most important for the area of the next cruise. Boat owners also swap charts and still use editions which were printed some years ago. This means that many yacht charts are only an approximation in their own right. Indeed, the publishers themselves will only guarantee some

The superb KVH Datascope.

charts to an accuracy of 0.1 nautical miles. The chart is only one navigational tool, just like the others on the table, and must be used in conjunction with them. Use the chart to back up your eyes and use a number of navaids to back up the chart.

Exercise 13.3

You are entering a strange harbour at night, and where you had expected to see the first of a series of green flashing lights, there is now a flashing white light (VQk F1 + LF1 10s). What conclusions do you draw and what would be your plan of action?

Back-Up Aids to Navigation Systems

My own boat is equipped with radar, but I would hate to be at sea without at least one form of sighting compass. Thanks to modern electronics, there is an emerging range of excellent devices built around a fluxgate compass incorporated into binoculars in such a way that the bearing is shown in digital form on an integral display. As you pan the device through an arc, so the bearing changes. Beyond binoculars, there is also a growing selection of 'data' machines which offer more than just a compass read-out. If your finances run to a Datascope-style back-up, you will increase both your navigational efficiency and versatility. The KVH equipment outlined below is typical and its uses are numerous.

The Datascope

This navaid is a combined monocular, sighting compass, emergency compass, range-finder, stop-watch and clock, designed to be gripped easily for one-hand operation and to have its functions controlled by combination pushes on the top mounted buttons – a bit like a trumpet player uses valves. The combinations are logical and easy to learn.

The monocular is of 5× magnification and can be focused. This enlargement is adequate for ninety per cent of cruising boat uses, but the binocular equivalents magnify seven or eight times which is about the maximum suitable for a small boat. With anything more powerful, the field of view becomes so small that it is difficult to hold it within the frame.

The sighting compass is quite brilliant. As soon as the Datascope is switched on, you see a very clear vertical line on screen, with the direction in which you are pointing displayed in large clear digits (this is important if you are like two-thirds of the population and need spectacles). To reinforce the approximation theme, the cardinal or semi-cardinal direction (N, NE, E, SE and so on) is also on show.

Being a full fluxgate compass, the

The Datascope as a sighting compass.

The Datascope in range-finder mode.

numbers settle in a millisecond with no compass card swing and they can be accurate to a fraction of a degree. Modern fluxgates are well damped and, unlike their predecessors, are inhibited against inaccuracy caused by tilt or end to end pitch and roll.

When in use, nine separate bearings can be recorded and recalled to show the time at which they were taken. On the boat, this is a super function for backing up radar. If the screen shows a target 30° off the boat's head, which is on 090, you swing the monocular until 120 shows and you should have the echo in enlarged picture. (Trying to do this by guesswork is not very effective.) Equally, if you don't have radar

you can track a ship which might be a problem and get a good record of its course. This will govern your action, following the rule that if a vessel is getting closer, but if its relative bearing to you remains constant, a collision is inevitable.

It also often happens that the radar shows three ships approaching and that one of them may become a hazard. With the eye, it is sometimes difficult to pick out the one which the radar is warning of, especially if it is slanting up from astern. The Datascope is of great help here. At night, most similar instruments have a night light, and this aspect really shows how good the Datascope is. Normally, a navigator locates a lighthouse or buoy, counts the flashes, times the period, then puts on spectacles to read the dial of the digital watch. With a scope you can do this all in one operation.

An integral marine range-finder works when the operator keys in (with the trumpet buttons) an object's known height – for example, a lighthouse from the chart or a beacon. With this target in view the buttons manipulate a bar graph to match its height and the instrument displays its range or how far off it is. Because this is a straight trigonometrical function, you could turn the scope on its side and key in a known length to reach the same answer. If, for instance, you were to measure the distance between two buoys or flagstaffs on the chart, this function could be used in lateral mode to let you know how far off they are.

The clock and stop-watch is as accurate as all other digital watch technology and has many on-board functions. This is the beauty of compass binoculars, or the Datascope and its derivatives; they make life much easier and are so simple to use that a lively skipper will use them very often. In turn, this will make him a better boat manager because sea safety is very much a matter of having the maximum amount of information at your fingertips.

Modern Navigation Instruments

These deserve the highest possible praise for the sheer volume of data they are able to offer the navigator via displays which are both clear and easy to read, and through computer-style menus which are simple to understand and to operate. My ideal navigation area would comprise a solid autopilot from a specialist company, but with pilot-house and cockpit controls and a separate compass read-out showing the boat's head in three-figure notation. I would also choose an analogue pointer showing how much the head is off course. By keeping the needle centralized, you know that you are bang on track, and in close manoeuvring, the needle acts as an indicator to remind you how the rudder is set.

Echo-Sounder

This would probably be my next most important tool in my ideal boat, because if there is a sensation worse than not knowing how much water is left under the keel, I do not want to know about it! The best echo-sounders have a digital indication of depth plus a video display of the contours of the sea-bed. You can have this on separate, switchable screens, or on a single split version. When you are negotiating an estuary, or creeping into a strange anchorage, this dual instrument shows the shape of the sand patches and the rocks and enables you to site the anchor where it is able to dig in, or even pull back into a small ledge.

GPS Navigator

A GPS navigator would come next on my list. It would have all the functions on a changeable combination of screens, enabling the operator to choose which cocktail he prefers.

Exercise 13.4

Do you understand GPS/Decca language? Test your knowledge of the abbreviations below and what they mean.

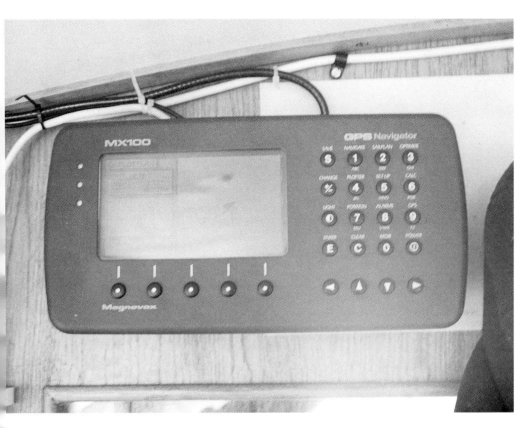

The C-Net GPS display.

1.	GPS.	6.	ETA.
2.	CTS.	7.	VMG.
3.	XTE.	8.	BRG.
4.	CMG.	9.	HDOP.
5.	SOG.	10.	NMEA.

Speed and Distance Log

This diminishes in importance because more accurate data is put out by GPS. It is, however, useful to watch how fast you run when you surf down waves and to be able to calculate the rate of current running against you. A log will give you a stored maximum speed and calculate your average speed since it was last reset. My own log also keeps a record of engine hours, so I know when to change oil and engine filters.

Combination Instrument

This can show all the data on one menu-driven display which could be used as a repeater on a flybridge, out in a cockpit, or down in a dry navigation area.

Wind Indicator

This instrument is a must on a cruising or

The chart plotter is the way ahead.

racing yacht. The most modern boats have clear screens and show both true wind and apparent wind (wind as its angle is affected by boat speed and sail set). The instrument can be calibrated for wind speed if you have a reference unit, but also has a remarkable feature whereby if you put the wind vane askew on the mast during installation, you can correct the error electronically from the keyboard.

All this information can be packed into some incredibly small black boxes. If you then add Weatherfax charts which can be plucked out of the air on to a notebook computer by an ordinary radio, and radars which can double up as echo-sounders,

GPS displays or an electronic charts, you have to agree that we navigators live in very exciting times.

The Chart Plotter

This is perhaps the most exciting piece of equipment available at the moment, with its ability to condense the ninety-six charts of the Balearic Islands into one credit-card sized cartridge. Unfortunately, the small size of the television-style screen means that if it shows all the detail of an Admiralty chart simultaneously then it is too cluttered to read. This could be very dangerous, but it brings our wheel full circle back to basics. Only a navigator who can choose some detail and is able to get information from a variety of sources will get the most from such expensive instruments.

You can spend a fortune on a boat's equipment, but the only safe sailor will be the one who has sufficient navigational expertise to pull all the data together and to spot immediately when a simple typing error could be about to cause a night-time catastrophe or a fog-aggravated shipwreck.

That should not now be a problem for you. Welcome to the club!

Weather Lore

On any cruising boat the weather is the most frequent anxiety and topic of conversation. Ancient weather observation has given rise to many rhymes which are useful (and sometimes very accurate) weather forecast devices.

Rainbow at night is the sailor's
    delight,
Rainbow at morning, sailor take
    warning.

Mackerel skies and mares' tails
Make tall ships carry short sails.

When the porpoise jumps
Stand by your pumps.

Seagull, seagull, sit on the sand,
It's never good weather when you're
    on the land.

When rain comes before the wind
Stays and topsails you must mind.
But with the wind before the rain
Your topsails you may set again.

When the wind shifts against the sun
Trust it not, for back it will run.
When the wind follows the sun
Fine weather will never be done.

If the wind is north east, three days
    without rain
Eight days will pass before south
    winds again.

ANSWERS TO EXERCISES

Chapter 2

Exercise 2.1

NE = 045; E = 090; SE = 135; S = 180; SW = 225; W = 270; NW = 315; ENE = 68; SSW = 203; NNW = 293.

Exercise 2.2

1. 030°.   4. 250°.
2. 055°.   5. 320°.
3. 140°.

Exercise 2.3

1. = zero three zero.
2. = zero five five.
3. = one four zero.
4. = two five zero.
5. = three two zero.

Exercise 2.4

1. Can buoy = 280.
2. Starboard marker = 295.
3. Lighthouse = 350.
4. Safe-water mark = 305.
6. Port-hand marker = 030.
7. Anchorage = 050.
8. Position fix = 080.

Exercise 2.5

1. 100M.   6. 187M.
2. 038M.   7. 338M.
3. 236M.   8. 066M.
4. 010M (magnetic north).   9. 128M.
5. 008M.   10. 116M.

Exercise 2.6

1. 187M.   6. 150M.
2. 308M.   7. 126M.
3. 338M.   8. 013M.
4. 200M.   9. 218M.
5. 277M.   10. 006M.

Exercise 2.7

1. 001T.   6. 178T.
2. 020T.   7. 195T.
3. 200T.   8. 252M.
4. 155M.   9. 047T.
5. 095M.   10. 320T.

Chapter 3

Exercise 3.1

1. As given in the main text.
2. Green cone, leave close to starboard.
3. Green triangle on pole, leave fair distance to starboard.

4. Red basket on pole, opposite number three. Split the distance between them.

5. Red can buoy. Leave well off to port.

6. Green cone, cut sharp around with this one on the starboard hand.

7. Red basket on pole, opposite number six. Head almost due south towards the end green stake.

8. A line of green perches. Turn to port and leave them close to starboard.

9. A line of red stakes. Leave them wide to port.

10. Green triangle on a stake. Leave to starboard and head towards the left-hand tree, then come on a reciprocal for the next buoy.

11. Green cone in line with the church. Go 90 degrees to port just short of it and pick up the next on about 070.

12. Safe-water mark. Two balls on red and white stake. Pass close either side.

Exercise 3.2

1. East.	6. South.
2. South.	7. West.
3. North.	8. South.
4. South.	9. North.
5. North.	10. East.

Exercise 3.3

1. YBY.
2. Two triangles pointing upwards.
3. Quick flashing (6) 10 seconds.
4. BYB.
5. YB.
6. Two triangles point to point.
7. Quick flashing (3) 5 seconds.
8. BY.
9. Quick flashing (9) 15 seconds.
10. Two triangles pointing downwards.

Exercise 3.4

1. Approximately 020T.
2. Approximately 320T.
3. Approximately 210T.
4. Approximately 275T.
5. YBY and quick flashing (9) 15 seconds.

Exercise 3.5

1. Anchorage.	7. E mark.
2. Lighthouse.	8. Starboard mark.
3. Isolated danger mark.	9. Underwater rock.
4. South mark.	10. Radar beacon.
5. Ship going	
6. N mark.	

Exercise 3.6

1. 50.24.00N 01.03.82W.
2. 50.24.75N 01.02.80W.
3. 50.23.60N 01.02.50W.
4. 50.23.90N 01.02.20W.
5. 50.22.00N 01.01.60W.
6. 50.21.95N 01.02.45W.
7. 50.21.30N 01.02.45W.
8. 50.21.00N 01.03.35W.
9. 50.20.90N 01.02.44W.
10. 50.20.60N 01.03.43W.

Exercise 3.7

1. 1.1nm.	4. 5.0nm.
2. 2.0nm.	5. 2.5nm.
3. 1.5nm.	

Exercise 3.8

1. 1.0nm.	4. 5.25nm.
2. 1.5nm.	5. 3.3nm.
3. 1.0nm.	

Exercise 3.9

1. 355T, 1.7nm.
2. 050T, 2.5nm.
3. 290T, 5.0nm.
4. 095T, 0.9nm.
5. 300T, 4.9nm.

Exercise 3.10

1. 50.29.75N 01.02.55W.
2. 50.29.00N 01.08.60W.
3. 50.27.15N 01.06.90W.
4. 50.27.75N 01.01.50W.
5. 50.26.80N 01.04.50W.
6. 50.24.10N 01.04.40W.
7. 50.25.25N 01.06.70W.
8. 50.24.80N 01.09.00W.
9. 50.23.10N 01.08.50W.
10. 50.21.75N 01.08.70W.

Exercise 3.11

		Course	Distance
1.	S–WP1	250	5nm
2.	WP1–WP2	160	2nm
3.	WP2–WP3	080	4.75nm
4.	WP3–WP4	240	2.25nm
5.	WP4–WP5	170	2.5nm
6.	WP5–WP6	310	2nm
7.	WP6–WP7	245	1.5nm
8.	WP7–WP8	175	1.6nm
9.	WP8–F	185	1.7nm

Exercise 3.12

1. 2 hours.
2. 12 minutes.
3. 1 hour 36 minutes.
4. 9 minutes.
5. 26 hours 48 minutes.
6. 13 hours 24 minutes.
7. 6 hours 36 minutes.
8. 1 hour 12 minutes.
9. 9 hours 24 minutes.
10. 2 hours 30 minutes.

Exercise 3.13

1. 10.81nm.
2. 8.3kn.
3. 2.5kn.
4. 29.3 hours.
5. 86nm.
6. 5.3kn.
7. 0.6kn.
8. 4.6kn.
9. 6kn.
10. 5.75kn.

Chapter 4

Exercise 4.1

1. Berry Head has two white flashes over a period of 15 seconds from a 58m tower. Its visibility is 18 miles.
2. Start Point Light's characteristics are three white flashes in 10 seconds. Range is 12 miles; also a fixed red with 12 mile range.
3. Les Hanois shows two quick flashes over a 5-second phase; range is 23 miles.
4. La Corbière has equal periods of red and white light over a 10-second span. It is 18m above sea level and has a 16-mile range.
5. Portsall has very quick, nine flashes occurring every 10 seconds. This makes it a slightly unusual west cardinal mark. This will be confirmed by the low height above sea level and the reduced range. It also has a radar reflector.

Exercise 4.2

1. Lt = light.
2. Bu = blue.
3. BRB = black, red, black.
4. Al = alternating.
5. Bn = beacon.
6. Tr = tower.
7. Y = yellow.
8. Iso = isophase.
9. Fs = flagstaff.
10. PA = position approximate.

Chapter 5

Exercise 5.1

	Day One	Day Two	Day Three	Day Four	Day Five
A.M.	2.6m	2.4m	4.4m	3.9m	4.5m
P.M.	1.9m	1.9m	4.1m	3.7m	4.9m
Mean	2.3m	2.1m	4.2m	3.8m	4.7m

Table 7.

Exercise 5.2

1.	1.3m.	6.	2.0m.
2.	1.2m.	7.	3.4m.
3.	3.0m.	8.	8.0m.
4.	4.1m.	9.	7.0m.
5.	7.4m.	10.	3.2m.

Exercise 5.3

Tuesday 10

10.30	11.30	12.30	13.30
0.3m	0.6m	0.9m	1.9m

14.30	15.30	16.30
2.9m	3.5m	4.1m

Tuesday 17

12.30	13.30	14.30	15.30
0.3m	0.6m	1.2m	2.1m

16.30	17.30	18.30
3.2m	4.2m	5.1m

Exercise 5.4

Day One	Day Two	Day Three
14.15	13.30	20.15

Day Four	Day Five
09.00	16.30

Chapter 6

Exercise 6.1

1. Approximately 085T.
2. Approximately 070T.
3. Approximately 067T.
4. Approximately 062T.
5. Approximately 060T.

Chapter 8

Exercise 8.1

1. Course is correct but distance is wrong.
2. Co-ordinates are correctly numbered, but should be W not E.
3. Not a S mark but a special buoy (colour yellow), and the longitude is wrong.
4. Information is correct.
5. The distance is obviously wrong if you look at the latitude scale. The upper case letter M means magnetic, not nautical miles (nm).
6. Waypoint is correct, but it could have been moved slightly to use the lines on the chart which would have given the simpler figures 50.31.00N 03.02.00W.
7. Waypoint is correct but unnecessary.

117

You could steam down the 0.03 line and then go due W along the 30N line straight to WP08. You can eyeball a course clear of the rocks.

8. Correct and well-chosen waypoint.

9. Approximately 0.5nm – not measured, but guessed off the chart matrix.

10. It has a radar reflector.

11. 030T/03nm – estimated off the chart, there is no need to measure.

12. 50.34.50N 03.07.00W. Notice that whole numbers are used where possible.

13. It uses simple numbers and will let you steam straight up the 03.10 line due N. It makes chartwork and posfixing easy.

14. 50.38.50N 03.10.00W.

15. Either a west cardinal or a cone/triangle starboard mark.

Chapter 9

Exercise 9.1

1. Approximately 05.30.
2. UTC/GMT – add 01.00 for BST.
3. 4.4m.
4. Plus.
5. + 00.50.
6. 05.30 + 00.50 = 06.20.
7. 0.28m.
8. 09.00 UTC.
9. Call either the harbourmaster or another yacht.
10. Steer on leading lights 296T. Occ 8s.

Exercise 9.2

1. 132 Deg True.
2. 22nm.
3. Measure it on the chart, or get it from Decca or another electronic navigator.
4. Angle the boat into Lyme Bay.
5. To avoid contra ebb tide further out.

6. Approximately 4 hours 30 mins (Allow 5 hours.)

7. ETA is HW Dev – 02.00 Depar about 10.30 to 10.45.

8. Approximately 6 knots.

9. At about 18.00.

10. Call the harbourmaster by telephone

11. Flashing four in 20 seconds from 43m tower. Range 29 miles. Also red ligh to guard the Shambles.

12. 4m plus the day's range (+ 8m).

13. Lobster-pot markers.

14. The Shambles well to the east, and warships from Portland.

15. Big ships and hydrofoil, coming and going.

Chapter 10

Exercise 10.1

1. Alter course to the south.
2. Pass either side of B. Give earl indication of intent, and sound your horn
3. Slow down. Pass under B's stern Speed up again.
4. Alter course to the east.
5. Alter course to the east or slow to le B pass ahead.
6. Stand on, but be wary.
7. Turn north. Accept that B is o wrong side of harbour entrance.
8. Slow down and turn south-east.
9. Leave a wide margin for safety whe going around big ship.
10. Alter course astern to north.

Exercise 10.2

1. Alter course to north.
2. Stand on. Maintain speed.
3. Stand on. It would be a courtesy t speed up when A turns south.

4. Stand on.
5. Stand on.
6. Alter course to north.
7. Stand on.
8. Emergency stop. Be ashamed of exit error.
9. Give a wide berth when rounding anchored vessel.
10. Alter course to north.

Exercise 10.3

1. ·
2. · · ·
3. ——
4. · ·
5. — — ·
6. · · · · ·
7. — — · ·
8. · · · pause ·
9. — — · ·
10. ·

Exercise 10.4

1. ·
2. · · · but A should have looked before going astern.
3. ——
4. None.
5. — · — ·
6. Probably none.
7. — · — ·
8. · · · pause ·
9. · · · · ·
10. None.

Chapter 11

Exercise 11.1

1. 1.5m.
2. 29 hours approximately.
3. 1 hour.

4. 12.00.
5. Any time after 20.00.
6. Allow 36 hours for the leg.
7. HM Coastguard by telephone or VHF.
8. Yacht *Valda*, 30ft motor-sailer ketch, colour green and white, sail number 1234, leaving Lyme Regis at this time, destination Audierne South Brittany, ETA 20.00 Tuesday, two persons on board.
9. HM Customs and Excise on appropriate form, harbourmaster who might need to use your berth, and your insurance company because most policies are invalid south of Brest.
10. 22.00.

Exercise 11.2

1. 210T.
2. 215M.
3. Port side.
4. Approx 8 hours after departure.
5. Avoid in plenty of time.
6. Start Point; Ile Vierge; Le Stiff/Ushant.
7. West Cardinal.
8. YBY; cones with points together; flashing 9.
9. 1 hour before HW Brest.
10. Approx 1330.

Exercise 11.3

La Valbelle	Red tower	Close port
CSE 190T	Distance 05nm	Time 43 minutes
Les Platresses	Green buoy	0.25nm Stbd
CSE 155T	Distance 1.7nm	Time 15 minutes

			ship's register, insurance documents,
Saint Paul	Red tower	Close port	ship's radio licence, radio operator's
CSE 170T	Distance	Time	licence, and possibly a VAT receipt.
	1.7nm	15 minutes	

3. Passport and medical insurance.

Saint Pierre	Green tower	0.5nm Stbd
CSE 180T	Distance	Time
	1.1nm	10 minutes

4. Regular broadcasts from HM Coastguard, coast radio stations, the BBC and so on.

Grand	Red tower	200m Port
Vinotière	Distance	Time
CSE 167T	2.75nm	24 minutes

5. There is no radio, you must telephone.

6. Generally, the harbourmaster will.

Fourmi	Green buoy	Close stbd
CSE 165T	Distance	Time
	4.0nm	35 minutes

7. Customs, Immigration, Affaires Maritimes (or none of them), cash collector for berthing fee.

8. The engine time is roughly 20 hours, burning 45–53 litres (10–12 gallons).

Vandrée	YBY	400m Port
CSE 172T	Distance	Time
	12.75nm	105 minutes

9. No, this is not obligatory in France unless you want a visit.

10. The ensign of your country of origin.

La Plate	YBY	50m Port

Chapter 13

Exercise 11.4

1. YBY.
2. Go into Baie des Trepasses and anchor until next slack water.
3. Rock with 3.6m water over it at LAT.
4. 105T and 8nm.
5. Approximately 20.30.
6. Generally, with you.
7. Approximately 23.00.
8. The seaward marks are E and W markers of rock, the inshore marker indicates rocks near beach.
9. Shallow patch just beyond the second light.
10. Pontoon.

Exercise 11.5

1. HM Customs form C1328 to be completed and left in box at quay.
2. Registration certificate or small

Exercise 13.1

1.	20.30.	6.	22.30.
2.	05.00.	7.	09.00.
3.	16.00.	8.	09.00.
4.	15.20.	9.	17.15.
5.	17.30.	10.	05.00.

Exercise 13.2

All of these ranges are approximate figures

1.	5.50m.	6.	4.50m.
2.	6.50m.	7.	2.50m.
3.	3.10m.	8.	5.75m.
4.	4.25m.	9.	5.75m.
5.	4.25m.	10.	5.50m.

Exercise 13.3

1. Settle the boat to a speed where you know you are not running into any danger

2. Double-check the characteristics of the light.

3. Get the best possible posfix from GPS and so on, or by bearings on other known lights or marks.

4. Check the bearing (and if possible the distance) from the problem light to your own position. If the bearing and distance roughly equate with the position where you expected the first green, it is possible that the harbour authority has decided to mark the entrance to the channel with a south cardinal buoy. The echo-sounder and the presence of other marks should also be helpful.

Exercise 13.4

1. Global Positioning System.

2. Course to steer – to go directly to a waypoint (WP).

3. Cross-track error – the distance you are off the straight (rhumb) line between WPs.

4. Course made good – the track the boat is actually following and which might be very different from where the nose is pointing. Sometimes called COG or course over ground.

5. Speed over ground – a contrary tide will make a log paddle wheel go faster and give an exaggerated speed reading. SOG is generally GPS derived and is generally a more useful reading than apparent speed through the water.

6. Estimated time of arrival – either at next WP, or at the final destination.

7. Velocity made good – the speed at which you are actually closing the target when the sideways component of travel has been rationalized.

8. Bearing – compass direction of next WP.

9. Horizontal dilution of position – an imprecise GPS position fix because the present distribution of the available satellites is giving a long, thin 'cocked hat'.

10. National Marine Electronic Association – agreed forms of protocol for the way in which information on all the above is passed from one piece of equipment to another. It is a bit like computer or fax modem language.

Measurements

Mariners have always used their own, traditional measurements. Below are some of the more usual.

6 feet	= 1 fathom
120 fathoms	= 1 cable length
7.5 cable lengths	= 1 shore mile
5280 ft	= 1 land mile
6076.1 ft	= 1 nautical mile
880 fathoms	= 1 sea mile
A ship's cable	= 720 ft
A hair's breadth	= $\frac{1}{48}$th of a degree
A nautical mile	= 1 degree

GLOSSARY

Alpha Computer style abbreviation signifying a navigation system's ability to accept instructions and titles in letters (in addition to figures).

Analogue Navigational information displayed and quantified using a pointer and scale.

Angular Distance A navigational convention agreeing that one degree of elevation from the Equator shall be equal to sixty nautical miles of 6,080 feet.

Azimuth Vertical angular distance usually measured from due South. In common parlance it is taken to mean height and angle above the horizon.

Bar The European unit of atmospheric pressure.

Bearing The relation of an object to the observer's own position, usually given as a compass bearing.

Breton Plotter A proprietary navigational instrument devised to make the measurement of courses and distances plotted on a chart a very simple operation.

Chart Plotter An electronic device which projects a marine chart onto a television-style screen and traces the ship's position and course on it. Most plotters also display all other electronically derived navigational information.

Clutter The radar interference caused by echoes being returned from breaking wave crests. Shows as a confusion of images at the centre of the radar display. Reduced and removed by a special control.

Contour A chart line linking points o similar seabed depth – usually drawn at 5 10 and 20 metres at LAT.

CPA Closest Point of Approach is a rada plotting term, being the estimated or pro jected closest distance which a target wil pass in relation to the observer's vessel i all speeds and headings remain constant.

Dead Reckoning The system of positio fixing calculated from observations of th boat's speed, heading, tide drift anc leeway.

Decca A radio navigation system base on fixed transmitters grouped in relate quartets of a Master and three Slave usually designated red, purple and green

Deviation More accurately called com pass deviation. The amount by which compass is in error from the real headin or angle from north.

Differential GPS A system which re moves the deliberate inaccuracy intro duced into GPS by the engineers. Depend on a receiver at a precisely known locatio calculating the GPS errors and sendin corrections to the ship via a radio link.

Dip The vertical angle at which th Earth's lines of magnetic force intersect it surface. Varies according to hemisphere.

Drying Height The height above se level attained by any hazard or land mas at LAT.

EBL Electronic Bearing Line on a radar, showing a target's angle relative to the ship's own position and heading.

EP An estimated position based on observation and informed guesswork. Usually plotted on the chart as a dot inside a triangle.

Ephemeris A table giving the present and future position (traditionally of a planet) of a GPS satellite.

Fathom An outmoded measurement of depth equal to six feet. Still seen on very old charts.

Fish Finder The name given to the sort of echo sounder which displays a special symbol when it detects the air in the swim bladder of a fin fish.

Fixed Errors A Decca term quantifying the amount of error at a particular location caused by signal distortion created by such effects as land/sea boundaries.

Fluxgate The term used to describe an electronic compass which derives its heading information from the proportional changes in induced voltage as a flux or toroid rotates across the earth's lines of magnetic force.

Gnomic Projection Is the chart drawing whereby a flat representation is presumed to touch the Earth at one point only. Gnomic is the lesser of the two common chart forms.

GPS Abbreviation for the US Dept of Defense Navstar Global Positioning System of navigational information derived from satellites and a computer radio receiver.

HDOP Horizontal Dilution of Precision, or the imprecision caused by a triangle of satellites not being in the ideal geometric alignment to give a very small positional area.

Hydrographer The Hydrographer to the Navy is the senior officer commanding the Admiralty service responsible for making surveys and producing charts.

IALA International Association of Lighthouse Authorities, whose work chiefly affects mariners in matters relating to buoyage and lighthouse descriptive conventions marked on charts.

LAT Lowest Astronomical Tide, or the lowest recorded tide level and usually the datum point from which depths quoted on the chart are taken. This means that there will always be at least the indicated amount of water at the relevant point.

Latitude The angular distance of any place measured along a meridian drawn North/South between the Equator and a Pole.

Lay Lines The closest angle to the wind which a sailing vessel must travel in order to reach a particular destination.

Log Sometimes taken to mean the book in which passage and other ship information is recorded and at others the machine or device used to record a ship's speed and distance travelled.

Longitude The angular measurement between a location's meridian and the meridian of Greenwich.

Loran An American-devised system of radio position fixing similar to Decca but having a greater range.

Lubber Line The fixed line on a compass bowl which shows exactly where the bow is pointing. Originally devised to make steering easier for a land lubber.

Mercator The most usual chart projection whereby the shape of the earth is projected onto a cylinder.

MF Medium frequency, or the radio band used for long-distance marine transmissions.

MHWN Mean High Water Neaps or the average height to which the tide rises near the time of the Moon's quarters.

MHWS Mean High Water Springs or the average height of Spring Tide observed over a period of years.

Nautical Mile A very precise distance of 6,080 feet.

Neap The tide at its smallest ranges.

NMEA National Marine Electronic Association or the computer language enabling marine instruments to speak a common protocol for the exchange of information.

Numeric In marine terms means the ability to accept information in statistical (as opposed to letter) form.

Period The time taken for a light to cover its flashing or occulting range and return to the start point.

Pixel One of the many elements making up a graphic image on a display.

Point A compass point is one of the 32 segments into which the compass was traditionally split, eg north north east by east.

Pseudo Random Codes Are the complex signal patterns sent out by GPS satellites in a form which the ship's receiver can translate into a very precise time of transmission.

Racon A device which is triggered by a received radio signal to transmit an enhanced echo back to the ship. Usually found on important buoys or beacons.

Reciprocal A bearing diametrically opposed to the one under consideration.

Rhumb Line A line drawn on the chart to cut parallel and meridians at the same

angle. In marine parlance usually taken to mean the straight line distance between two points.

S/A Selective Availability, or the engineer's deliberately induced diminution of GPS precision. Normally a circle of 100-metre diameter.

Separation Zone Obligatory channels around busy sea areas designed to separate ships heading in opposite directions by a 'no go' corridor of several miles width.

Spikes Irregularities in voltage. Can cause problems in delicate electronic apparatus.

Spring Tide Is a relatively large rise and fall occurring near the Moon's New and Full phases.

Squelch The radio control which is set to eliminate white noise created by the radio's own circuitry and allowing the reception of signals stronger than the acceptance threshold.

SSB Single Sideband where only one half of the sine wave output is transmitted thereby giving it greater thrust.

Tidal Range The daily difference between the heights of high water and low water.

Transducer A device like a microphone which converts one sort of energy into another.

Transit The straight line drawn between two identifiable fixed locations.

UT Universal Time, which is the term slowly replacing Greenwich Mean Time.

Variation Magnetic Variation, or the varying amount by which the compass display will differ from True North.

VHF Very High Frequency, or the band which is used for short distance marine communications. It begins at 156.00 Megahertz (Channel Zero) and is stepped up in 25 Khz segments, each given a number.

VRM Variable Range Marker – the adjustable electronic circle drawn around the centre point of a radar screen and varied to show the distance of an echo from it.

INDEX

(Page numbers in italics refer to illustrations)

Admiralty: chart 5011, 22
  practice charts, 6
  Tide Tables, 44
Alderney race, 60
analogue pointer, 110
angular distance, 30–1
anti-collision rules, 81–5
astro-navigation, 101
Audierne, 87, 93, 98
  chartlet, 95
  route to, 86
autopilot, 71, 110

beacons, lighted, 40, 41
bearing, 9, 13
  hand, 25
  see also reciprocal bearings
boat specifications, 90
box the compass, 9
Breton plotter, 14, 26
buoyage, 22–5, 44
  IALA, 23–4
  symbols, 39
buoys, 39
  colour codings, 24, 39
  mooring, 40

cardinal points, 8, 9
  half, 8 9
channel indicators, 23
chartlets, 44, 92, 94, 95
  Cabo Gitano, 75
  tide, use of, 60–1
chart plotter, 112
charts, 16, 21–37, 89, 96–8
  availability, 90
  corrections, 106–7
  depth contours, 40, 41
  pilots, 5

study of, 39
symbols, 21, 22
  see also Admiralty charts
Chartwork approximation, 105–6
CMG, course made good, 55, 66
COG, course over the ground, 55
collision: rules for avoiding, 81–5
colours (buoys), 24
combination instrument, 111
compass angle: measuring, 11–19
compass, 7–20, 103
  360-degree notation, 9
  deviation, 18–19
  card, 18
  early, 8
  hand held, 12, 25
  magnetic, 8
  terminology, 8–10
compass rose, 10
conversions of units, approximate, 103
Cotentin Peninsula, 53
course: deviation 53–5, 61
  laying, 34–6
CTS, course to steer, 56–9, 66

day book, 69
Decca radio navigator, 5, 17, 27, 28, 54, 66, 69
  chains, 70
depth contours, 40, 41
depth-sounders, 5, 48
digital information: plotting from, 27–31
distance, of journey, 93
  log, 111

dividers, pair of: use of, 32

echo-sounder, 110, 112
electronic navigation, 68–75
  operator error, 71, 73
Enavigator (position-fixing) systems, 69, 71
  display, 71
estimated position: chart, 27
ETA, estimated time of arrival, 36–7, 80, 103

GPS, Global Positioning System, 5, 17, 27, 54, 66, 69, 103
  display, 29, 111
  navigator, 110
  satellite Birdcage, 70
Greenwich meridian, 30

hazards, 39–40
high water (HW): see tides

IALA, International Association of Lighthouse Authorities buoyage, 23–4
IMO, International Maritime Organisation, rules, 81
Imray charts, 6
  and tidal flow, 47

journey, planning, 59–61, 76–80, 86–100
  feasibility study, 87
  rough guide, 87–8

knots, 54
KVH datascope, 107, 108
  in range-finder mode, 109

LAT, Lowest Astronomical Tide, 44

teral marks, 23
titude, 27, 30, 32, 36, 60, 66, 73
e Chenal du Four, 91
  chart, 89
  chartlet, 92
ghthouses, 41–2
ghts (buoys), 24, 41–2
g book, 62–7
  author's log sheet, 63
  author's passage log, 64
  Cruising Association, 62
  sheet one, 64–6
  sheet two, 66–7
g impeller, 54
ngitude, 27, 30, 32, 36, 60, 66, 73
oran-C receivers, 27, 69
w water (LW): see tides
SP, log (indicated) speed, 55
yme Regis, 76, 96
  harbour, 77, 87
    plan of, 78

agnetic deviation, 15
agnetic north, 15

autical mile, 31
  measuring, 34
vigation: facts, 77
  instruments, modern, 110–13
systems, back-up aids to, 107–10
  see also electronic navigation
rth: magnetic, 15
  true, 15
tices to Mariners, 106

-setting course, 55–9
ertaking: rules for, 82

parallel rule: use of, 12–13, 26, 32
plotter, 29
  see also Breton plotter
plotting, practical, 11–14
  from digital information, 27–31
Portland Bill, 79
  cruise round, 76–80
  light, 43
  race, 76
  tide and counter-tide, 53
port marks, 22
Portsall, 96, 97
positional fix, 13, 27
position: fixing, by Enavigator system, 69, 71
  lighthouses, 41–2
  identifying, 25–7
protractor, circular, 12

radar, 5
radio, 5
Raz de Sein, 93, 97, 98
  chartlet, 94
reciprocal bearing, 17–18
reference cards, 38
rhumb-line course, 79
rhumb-line distance, 79
rocks, 40
roller ruler, 32
route planning, 34–6
Rule of Twelfths, 50–1, 105
rules, at sea, 81–5
running fix, 54

Shambles, The, 43
shipping forecasts, 64
SOG, speed over the ground, 55
sound signals, 84
speed, 36–7

calculation, 53–5
  log, 111
starboard marks, 22

tidal bulge, 45
tidal curve, 106
tidal diamonds, 44
tidal flow, 44, 46
  diagrams, 47, 58, 59
tidal heights, 47
tidal information, 78
tidal off-set diagram, 56
tidal range, 49
tides, 44–52, 88
  Admiralty tables, 44, 104
  approximations, 104–5
  British, reference, 59
  effect of, 52–61
  effect of sun and moon on, 45
  half, time of, 103
  information, 44, 91
  neap, 44, 47, 59
  race, 60
  spring, 44, 47, 59
time approximations, 103–4
true north, 15
turning points, 36

Ushant Traffic Separation Scheme, 88

waypoints, 36, 66, 73–4, 93
  book, 73
  Cabo Finisterre, 72
weatherfax charts, 112
weather recording sheet, 64, 65
Weymouth harbour, 80
wind indicator, 111–12
wrecks, 40

XTE, cross-track error, 55, 66